Jadlow:
On The Rebound

Todd Jadlow & Tom Brew

ISBN Number: 978-0-9858021-4-1

Hilltop30 Publishers, LLC
P.O. Box 973
Schererville, Indiana 46375

E-mail: tombrew@hilltop30.com

Website: www.Hilltop30.com

✶ ✶

To my five girls: Alexia, Adriana,
Sofia, Kiara and Camryn.
And to Jamie, my love.

For all those suffering souls both inside and outside of walls.
Always remember that no matter how bad things are or how dark
times get, there is always a way to rebound, recover, and change
the direction of that path we walk. May God bless you all!

–Todd Jadlow

For my favorite starting five:
My three children, Whitney, Ashley and Tyler,
and my two granddaughters, Kara and Penny.

And for the troubled souls who still suffer.

–Tom Brew

Jadlow: On The Rebound

TABLE OF CONTENTS

TABLE OF CONTENTS (Cont.)

Chapter

THE HIGHEST OF HIGHS
AND THE LOWEST OF LOWS

There is nothing better than this.

I've mentioned those words so many times during all my years of playing basketball. Whether it was growing up a star in a small town in Kansas, playing college basketball at the highest level at Indiana University in front of the greatest fans in the world or while I was playing professionally for a dozen years through the U.S., Europe and South America, that's always the way I've thought.

There is nothing better than this.

I never got to realize my full NBA dreams, even though they were just inches away from me, but I've never regretted that. Well, not too much. When it came to basketball, I really had a lot of fun. I've questioned a lot of my decisions through the years, but despite the occasional doubts, I have to say I had a great time all those years when I had a basketball in my hand.

I played in a lot of big games, in front of a lot of crazy fans. I was part of a national championship at Indiana in 1987 and got to spend four years with the legendary coach Bob Knight. I made more than a million dollars as a pro and won four championships in my decade-plus as a pro, playing in places like France, Belgium, Switzerland and Argentina. And I totally enjoyed all the things that came along with being a basketball star.

Fame.

Adulation.

Girls.

Drugs.

And many nights, all of the above.

There was lots of fame and adulation, especially at Indiana, where they are crazy about their college basketball and treated us players like rock stars in and around Bloomington. There were lots of girls, too, a whole lot. It was good to be a Hoosier. And as a pro, there were lots of girls and lots of drugs at my disposal. It didn't matter where I played, in the States, Europe or South America, the routine all those years was practically always the same. Play games, then party hard – really hard – with lots of cocaine and alcohol and women.

It became a way of life for me, and day after day and year after year, my partying and alcohol and drug use kept getting worse and worse. By 2013, here I was in my late 40s, and I was acting like an out-of-control kid. I would go days at a time getting drunk and high from the minute I woke up.

And why? Because I had reached that point where I didn't really care anymore. I had a bad case of saying "To Hell With It." After a bad car accident that caused severe neck and back pain and mental issues from a severe concussion, all my days were spent medicating myself – both legally and illegally – just to get through the day.

I was so out of control that I got four DUIs in six months, including two in one day. Two in one day? You're probably wondering how that is even possible, but I can tell you it was pretty easy. On two of my first three DUIs, I was back on the road within a few hours. Both times when I picked up my car, the drink that I had with me was still there.

Both times I gulped it down and drove on my merry way, without a care in the world. And every time, as soon as I got home, I poured myself another drink.

On the fourth DUI, I had pissed off the world so bad that they came after me with a vengeance. An ex-wife with a vendetta orchestrated a media blitz that humiliated me and raised ire so bad in the metro Kansas City area that I spent close to two years in jail for my wild times.

Imagine that. Everyone was so upset that I was driving down the highway at 121 miles per hour with a drink in my hand and too much alcohol in my body and my head. They were even more upset that I did it with my 2-year-old daughter in the back seat.

I didn't get the fuss.

But on that day, December 11th of 2013, they took me to jail. I spent day after day alone, hidden from the real world. I was angry and depressed and mad at the world. I was many things in my mind, but what I wasn't was a drug addict or an alcoholic. Nope, not me. Not Todd Jadlow, former basketball star. Not Todd Jadlow, successful businessman. Not Todd Jadlow, loyal father to five beautiful girls.

No, not me. Not Todd Jadlow.

Nothing better than this?

No, there was nothing worse than this.

I spent more than a year in jail just biding my time. I read, wrote in journals and kept to myself, my days broken up only by trips back and forth to court, dressed in orange jail garb and doing the shackle shuffle down the hallways of one courthouse after another, usually with TV cameras rolling.

The humiliation and shame was overwhelming. The only

That's me, Todd Jadlow (left), listening intently as Indiana coach Bob Knight goes over a few things during a game.

feelings that raced through my head were those of guilt, sadness and remorse. I just wanted to die and the feelings were overwhelming. It had come to this for a kid from Salina, Kansas who fought through constant teasing and hazing as a youngster because of my nervous tics, who had survived four years of physical and mental abuse from Bob Knight at Indiana, who had survived years and years of wild nights of parties and near-misses with the law, both behind the wheel and on the receiving end of major drug deals.

Mine was a life completely spun out of control.

Then one day a man came to speak to me and my 50 other incarcerated derelicts and he asked us all who had drug or alcohol problems. Everyone raised their hand.

Everyone but me.

Even after more than a year in jail and the loss of everything that mattered to me – my house, my cars, my money, my kids and mostly my self-esteem and reputation – I still didn't want to believe that I had a problem.

But he knew I had a problem. With a room full of troubled souls, he zeroed in on me. He yelled at me and called me out, this big hot-shot basketball star who thought he was above the world. It made me pretty angry that day, but a few days later I got his phone number from one of the guards and we started to talk. One conversation led to another and as the days and weeks passed, I learned a lot of things.

I learned, mostly, that drugs and alcohol weren't my problem. Todd's problem? Todd was Todd's problem, and the drugs and alcohol were mere masks to hide all that was wrong with me.

I've learned a lot about myself since that day nearly three years ago when I went to jail for good. What I learned that mattered the most is that I never want anyone to go through what I went through. Losing your head and losing your life through drugs

Here I am grabbing a rebound against Michigan during my senior year in 1989. IU beat Michigan twice that year but UM won the NCAA title.

and alcohol is something I wouldn't wish on anyone.

And now, it's up to me to do something about it. I want to help others, and in doing so I will help myself lead a promising road to recovery. I've been nearly three years clean from drugs and alcohol now and the best thing I can do for kids at high schools and colleges is to bare my soul and tell my story.

I tell it all, too, all the good and all the bad. It's part of my Todd Jadlow Give It Back Foundation where I go around to schools and universities to speak. My mission statement is simple, to reach one child, one person or one family and make a difference in their lives.

And in doing it, I make a difference in my own life as well. I don't want to live through all that craziness any more. I want a sound, safe normal life, where I can act like a human being and love on my daughters, and love on my girlfriend and get through every day and night without any craziness.

During this journey, I have found that recovery has allowed me to grow, mend, heal and – most importantly – allow me to get out in front of an audience and be a voice that tries to instill hope in others. No matter how low you go, or how hard you fall, there is always a way to get back up and recover.

Recovery has given me a purpose in life, and now my passion is to help others, even if it's just one person at a time. Recovery has allowed me to make peace with my past and has put a silver lining on my story. It has taught me how to be grateful in life, not only for all the good, but the bad as well.

I often say that if you can't find empathy in your heart for someone who is battling their issues, whether it's a person that has someone at home – be it a brother or sister, or father or mother – who has a broken heart and this person desperately wants them back, then you don't have feelings.

I want to help that person, and the person after that. And on and on. There are a lot of kids hurting out there.

I have a story to tell, one that will help that person one at a time. Mine is a story well worth telling, one filled with the highest of highs and the lowest of lows.

It's been quite a journey … and it's nowhere near over. When I give a speech and then get a heart-breaking letter from a kid in need, desperately searching for answers, it really affects me emotionally. I've opened a door to help that person, and that makes me feel so good.

The feeling? There is nothing better than this.

2

Chapter

GROWING UP JADLOW
IN SMALL-TOWN KANSAS

Plenty of kids have had tougher childhoods than I have, and a lot of have had it easier. But all I know is my childhood, and it was hard.

I had nervous tics as a kid and people made fun of me all the time. Everyone did, the neighbor kids, even the ones I thought were my friends. It was unmerciful at school. I remember being chased home several times as a kid, scared to death because the older kids wanted to beat me up. I could run fast and they couldn't catch me, but they tried on a daily basis. I can remember many, many days where I would sprint home with them on my tail as I lunged inside my house and locked the doors.

Even when I was successful at things as a kid, I got teased and bullied all the time because of my tics. I couldn't hide them and I certainly couldn't control them. I was an easy target, I guess. I was so competitive at things at school because I wanted to fit in and be liked. But it never really mattered when I was a little kid. No one ever liked me. We used to race around the courtyard circle to see who was the fastest in the class, and I always wanted to win so bad, just to impress my classmates. They still didn't like me.

I won my first Punt, Pass and Kick competition when I was

in the second grade and I was so excited. That trophy is perhaps the most prized trophy I own and I remember winning it like it was yesterday. I was extremely proud of winning, but I really couldn't share my joy with anybody. I was all alone because I didn't fit in with the "in" crowd. Even when I won that important competition,

 it still didn't matter because they teased me even worse after that. The mocking and the bullying were horrendous at that point, and I never told anyone about how much it hurt me because I was so embarrassed. I held every-thing in and developed extremely thick skin because of it. I vowed at an early age that I would show everyone later in life that I mattered. But at the time, when you're a little kid in a small town, it was really tough to go through. I spent a lot of nights crying myself to sleep in my bed.

***   ***   ***

The teasing and bullying didn't end with the kids at school. I had to put up with the teasing at home, too.

Even from my parents.

At home when I would be around my parents and get tics, they would get so mad at me and scream at me to stop doing those things. I would tell them I couldn't stop, but I would keep having them and they would keep yelling at me. I got no sympathy from them at all. It was bad enough being picked on by kids, but it's a thousand times worse when you don't get any compassion from your own parents. I hated that, and I felt so worthless. They had me teared up on the inside all the time. I tried not to show my emo-tions on the outside, but inside I just got ripped apart. The feeling was just too overwhelming. They would constantly get on me and say things to me, and they would get extremely angry with me because I could not stop it.

What were my tics like? They were terrible. I had one where I had to scrape my hands on the ground just to get them under control and when they came on, I would stop in the middle of running to do it. It is almost as if I had to feel the ground. I scraped my hands so often that they would get all calloused and bloody. Those impulses to do it were so strong that as bad as I didn't want to do it, I couldn't stop.

Another tic was making noises, like sharp grunts from my throat. It was horrible, especially when I was at school in the middle of a class and couldn't stop. Another one was jumping in the air and kicking my legs against my butt. It was a totally uncontrolled action. Want more? Another tic was flailing my arm upward hard at the elbow. I would also twitch my head and blink my eyes real hard.

Concentrating on not doing these things only made it worse. I tried extremely hard not to, but I couldn't do it. I used to lay in my bed at night and pray to God, "Please take these tics away, please I can't handle it, I can't handle all the teasing, and being made fun of and so forth." I spent a lot of time in my room with the door closed so I didn't have to put up with the ridicule at home as well. Home was supposed to be my safe haven, but it never was.

My mother finally took me to see Dr. Rosales because she thought I had Tourette's Syndrome. The doctor put me through a series of tests and interviews and said I didn't have Tourette's, that they were just nervous habits and that I would grow out of them as I got older. I spent every night praying for those tics to stop, because I just wanted to be a normal kid. The sound of that very word *tic* to this day makes me cringe.

The doctor prescribed Haldol for me, but it had a huge amount of side effects and made me lethargic and I felt that it interfered with my sports. I remember when I got prescribed the medication, I thought I was going to be normal, like all the other kids. The medicine did nothing, and it wasn't the magical potion I had hoped it would be. I was devastated that I still had these tics and kept reminding myself as a kid I will just grow out of it, like the doctor said. I couldn't grow up fast enough. The mocking and bullying had a huge impact on my life and it made me not trust people or believe in them. It created a "Me against the world" mentality and a deep sense of worthlessness.

*** *** ***

It wasn't just the tics. We were an awkward family, one that just coexisted. There was no love in my immediate family, that being my mother and father. There were no "I love you's" shared on a daily basis, or even at all. We were all just individuals under a roof and there was no love. I have never felt loved by my parents, nor did they ever convey love. This is why as an adult that I make it a point every day to tell my kids every chance I get that I love them.

To this day, 49 years later, my father has never once told me that he loved me. Not once!

My parents were different people. My mother was an office secretary and manager for a large trucking firm during most of her work career. My mother came from a large family with eight brothers. My father worked for Kansas Power & Light for over 30 years. He was a lineman and then a foreman for them. I guess you would call us a middle class family. I remember my young years in an apartment, and then in a rental home. My parents' first house they bought was down the street from my grade school and high school, and it cost them something like $18,000.

It was a nice split-level house with three bedrooms and two baths. My dad did a nice job of fixing it up. Downstairs we had a pot-belly fireplace that made the house toasty in the winter. I had two dogs growing up, a Chihuahua named Buffy and a Brittney hunting dog named Mike. They both lived outside and were not allowed in the house. My parents were rarely around. They worked all the time trying to make ends meet.

I remember as a kid there was never any food in my home and I was constantly starving. That's how I learned to cook at a young age. I would find anything I could and try to make something. Our biggest enjoyment came on Fridays and the hope that we could actually go out to eat. I remember I would clean the house spotless on Fridays, hoping that dinner out would be my reward for it. To go out to eat was a huge luxury for us, because it didn't happen very often. When we did, we would go eat at a Mexican restaurant called La Hacienda, and what a huge treat that was.

My father was involved in many activities and I usually tagged along when I was little. He played fast-pitch softball on a really good team and they traveled everywhere to play. He was a well- known pitcher who could really throw hard. He had this enormous reputation that proceeded him that made me very proud. My dad also was a trap-shooting champion and he traveled everywhere with my uncle doing trap shoots. That was always a fun time. My dad would often take me fishing and hunting, two things I loved to do. One thing about my dad though is that he was a man of few words. We rarely had conversations about anything and could sit hours without saying anything to each other. There was a bond, but not a loving bond. It was more of a peaceful coexistence.

*** *** ***

My mother came from a big family. She had eight brothers and she was the only female. She grew up in a two-bedroom house with all her brothers. My grandfather was a railroad engineer – he piloted the train – and my grandmother was a stay-at-home mom. She was truly an angel and the true definition of what a grandmother is. She was very loving, caring and nurturing and would do anything for you. She made incredible food and the family got together every Saturday at Grandma's to eat hamburgers and every Sunday after church to have breakfast.

It was fun to get to know my uncles so well. I spent a lot of time with my Uncle Dan, going to drag races because as he raced for Budweiser and that was a big deal. I developed my strong work ethic from my uncle Dave at early age by working for him drilling wells. He died of ALS, but he kept on working until he couldn't move any more. He fought the disease so hard and even at the end, he would run the well rig by leaning on the levers with his arms because he didn't have use of his hands. He was always so fun to be around. I didn't have a driver's license yet but he would still have me running this huge machinery and the water trucks and the well drilling rig. I was like 11 and 12 years old and I'm making $350 a week, which was a ton of money back then. He will to live and his work ethic got ingrained in me. He inspired me to give it your all and always fight to the end.

The other uncle I was close to was my Uncle Rick. He was the youngest of my mother's brothers and was a rocker, a drummer in famous rock bands. Later in life he became my party uncle, and we did a lot of cocaine together.

My grandfather drank daily and was drunk all the time.

My poor grandmother would have to put up with him throwing fits during drunken rages all the time. I remember once my grandfather didn't like the food she made, so he threw the potato soup at my grandmother. He was so drunk that he couldn't even walk. He was stumbling all over the place. The three things my grandfather did well was make moonshine in his still, drink whiskey and collect diamonds. My grandfather was an alcoholic and died from cirrhosis of the liver. He drank himself to death. My grandmother deserved better. She was a saint, and was very influential in my life.

My other uncles all owned their own businesses and were successful. One owned a Budweiser distributorship, so at every family function there was plenty of alcohol present – and in large volumes, from every type of Anheuser-Busch product to all sorts of whiskey. My family loved to drink and did a lot of it. Every family get-together was a drunk-fest.

As a kid, my mother was the person I identified with the most. She took me to all my sporting events, practices and games. I rarely remember my dad being at my practices and games. I was truly a Momma's boy. My dad just never said anything. And when I needed something, I asked my mom.

*** *** ***

We had very little money growing up, so everything I had, I cherished. I remember an incredible day was when my mom took me shopping to get some clothes and shoes. That was a huge deal, and we had so much fun. But I remember when we got home and she had to tell my dad she spent money on clothes for me, he got so angry. I can tell you that every pair of shoes I owned had holes in the soles and I would put cardboard in them or black tape to cover the holes. The outside of the shoes looked like new

15

because I would constantly clean them, but on the inside they were old and worn. I remember my socks were always soaked or had holes in them because of the holes in my shoes. I also had to tape up my socks at the top because they were so worn out there would be no elastic left to hold them up. That's how it was for me growing up. We had no money for anything considered a luxury.

Growing up in Salina, you had to make your own fun because it was a small community. I played every sport there was. I spent every free moment I had at the YMCA. I would even walk to and from there at one point and it was five miles away.

*** *** ***

I had all sorts of hobbies as a kid, and I loved them all. I learned to hunt and fish, and I did so every chance I got with my dad and the neighbor kids. I collected baseball cards, coins and stamps and had an uncle – my Uncle Glen – who had a huge coin collection and he always helped me out with the keys to my coin sets.

The keys are the rare coins that are expensive and there are only a few of them that were ever made or circulated. My Uncle Glen, every time I saw him would give me a key coin to my set. He also gave me several book sets, and I loved all that stuff. I also built RC airplanes as a kid and tried to fly them, and I launched rockets all the time too.

That stuff was fun, but it was all about sports for me. That's what I really loved. I played every sport there was and was good at them. I played basketball, baseball, track, and football. I bought my first dirt bike and loved riding that as much as I could.

We were always playing something. At night time the neighborhood kids and I would play some sport every day and we had some form of the Olympics many times within our neighbor-hood. I had dreams when I was a kid of playing for the Harlem Globetrotters and would practice daily thinking that maybe they would drive by and see me practicing. I was a dreamer.

Growing up as a kid in Salina, well, I can tell you it was quite an adventure.

3

Chapter

THE YOUNG CATHOLIC KID
GETTING A GOOD FOUNDATION

I was raised in a Catholic family, so I started school out at St. Mary's Grade School in Salina. I was comfortable there, at least as comfortable as I could be for all that was going on with me. But for junior high, my parents forced me to go to the public school – South Junior High – because they did not have the money to pay for a parochial education.

It was a tough transition for me. I struggled at South and begged my mom every day to let me to go back to the Catholic school where all my friends were. Sacred Heart Junior High was downtown by the cathedral and it cost money to get a parochial education. I was so unhappy that I finally told my parents that I was quitting school if they didn't let me go back to the school at Sacred Heart. I was used to really small classes at Sacred Heart and I hated the fact the Salina South was enormous. It was overwhelming for me.

Fortunately, my parents spoke with our church pastor and came to a financial agreement that would allow me to go back to a school with all my friends, and I was ecstatic. I remember walking into my first class back at Sacred Heart. It was a science class taught by Fritz Jaquay, and my best friend Kevin Simoneau was in the class. When I walked in he stood up and told everyone that now we were going to win the basketball championship.

Kevin was my best friend and was a neighbor of mine. He lived on Ralph Street and I lived on Carl, one block down. Moving back to the Catholic school was the best thing that ever happened to me in my early years. I loved it there and thrived there. I did really well in school as well with my grades. I still dealt with those kids that still decided to tease me because of my nervous tics, but I was getting older and they were getting better. I was one of the older kids now, too, and that helped.

Middle school for me was more about growing as a person and finding out who I was. I fit in really well in middle school at Sacred Heart, and it really was an important transition period of my life. My tics were still prevalent but I honestly wasn't teased and bullied as much there as I was in grade school. In middle school, I

I wasn't just a tall and skinny basketball player as a kid, I was also a tall and skinny football player, too. I loved all sorts of sports as a kid.

started to establish some pretty good friendships, and that made me feel more comfortable.

I also started my affinity for the love of girls about that time, which is where I had my first girlfriend, my first kiss and spent endless amounts of hours on the phone with them. It helped a lot that I was becoming more popular because of sports. I was 5-foot-10 as an eighth grader, which was tall back then. I was really good at a lot of sports too besides basketball. I played baseball and football, and I ran track. I remember it being a big deal when I could run and jump to touch the rim. I'm sure a lot of junior high kids dunk now, but back then it meant a lot to me just to get the rim.

During this time, I ws proud to be a Catholic. We started every day at school by going to mass in the morning at the cathedral across the street from the middle school. My devotion to God was strengthening and I was now truly forming a relationship with him. I loved my religion classes and excelled in them. God became a focal point in my life and I often prayed to him.

I'm glad I had that time at Sacred Heart. It set a good foundation for me.

TODD JADLOW & TOM BREW

22

Chapter

MY HIGH SCHOOL DAYS
AND RISING ABOVE THE BULLIES

Making the move from junior high to high school wasn't easy. I was thrilled to be heading off to Sacred Heart High School. It's where I wanted to go, for sure. They have a very rich tradition in athletics. They also have a rich tradition in hazing, bullying and intimidating the freshmen

A common practice at my school was "tanking" an individual. There was this huge basin in the bathroom that you washed your hands in. The upperclassmen would grab a weak kid in the hallway and take him into the bathroom and dunk him in the basin from head to toe. This would go on every day and the faculty did nothing about it. The kid would then walk around the rest of the day soaked, and it was humiliating.

They tried to get me once my freshman year. I fought with all my might and they didn't get me into the bathroom. The whole experience was terrifying and humiliating and the people that tried this on me were the popular athletes at the school. To me they were punks and cowards, and I couldn't stand them for doing that to people. The freshman guys were in fear on a daily basis because there was a ton of that kind of stuff that went on in the school.

Also at my school there was a lot of drug use. I remember

several kids in class sifting marijuana seeds on their desktops as the older nuns who taught the class would walk by and tell them to get that grass off their desks. They really did think it was grass from the outside. That's how naive they truly were about drugs, besides the fact they were extremely old and senile.

My tics were still a problem, and being around older kids again, I got mocked a lot, both in the hallways and outside at recess. I remember one nervous habit that I had of making a noise with my throat and we were all in gym class outside and running timed 40-yard sprints. When it was my turn to run, the whole bleacher section of kids – and there were probably 30 of them – starting mocking me in harmony as I was getting ready to run my sprint. I could hear them loud and clear as they made that sound I make. When I finished, I walked over to the bleachers and just stared down everyone. I had never been so humiliated in my life.

The whole class was mocking me and making fun at me. I just wanted to crawl under a rock and die, but I faced every one of those pricks and just dared them to say one thing to me. The teasing went on daily, and it was nonstop. It went on during lunch in the cafeteria, and even in the hallways between classes and so forth. It was almost unbearable and I was dying inside. I vowed that someday I would become successful and would be done with each and every one of them.

To this day, I have never been back for any class reunion or have spoken with any of them. There was too much pain from the experience of high school that freshman year. I was just a young freshman that year and they treated me that way. I even played football, basketball and ran track, but they still picked on me as much as they could.

And then things changed. As a sophomore I got an opportunity to start on the varsity basketball team, which was unheard of at a school like Sacred Heart, one so rich in athletic tradition with all the state championships they had won. As soon as I was placed into the starting lineup, I gained instant credibility with everyone at the school, and I was no longer made fun of, bullied or teased.

It stopped that fast. Literally overnight.

And all because I was suddenly a varsity basketball player. How lame.

Was this for real? That was the only thought that went through my mind. I was the same kid with the same nervous tics, but now I was treated completely differently because of my stature with the basketball team. I loved it, but it was all very confusing. Some of my friends at the time became jealous because of my accomplishments, but the teasing and mocking essentially ended. As a sophomore I started on the varsity football team as a punter. I also still played Babe Ruth baseball and was on the track team as well. I did well in school and I loved shop class, where I made several huge beautiful china hutches. It was a fun year, my first fun year really.

The end of my sophomore year, I went to a big basketball camp that put me on the map exposure-wise. My junior and senior years, we won a lot of games but we never won a state championship. I led the city in scoring both my junior and senior years, and I became very popular with college coaches from around the country. I was recruited by more than 200 schools.

*** *** ***

The first time I drank was as a freshman in high school, in the fall of 1980. I went with friends to a Klepper's gas station and bought malt duck and big mouth Mickey's, and we walked around with our Army trench coats on, with the pockets full of

25

Sacred Heart High School in Salina, Kansas has a great basketball tradition and I was glad to be a part of it. I loved playing there.

alcohol.

The first time I ever tried any drug was my sophomore year in 1981. I tried marijuana and hated it. Tony Betz was an upperclassmen at Sacred Heart, and he let me drive his hot Camaro one day and gave me a joint to smoke as well. After we smoked the joint and I was going home, he told me to go over to the neighbor's pine tree and grab some of the pine needles and rub them on my hands and clothes so my parents wouldn't smell the weed. So I did and went inside but my parents weren't around, of course. That first time I tried marijuana, it made me dizzy and nauseous. I was sick to my stomach, and I hated the feeling of my head spinning and not feeling in control. I didn't have any interest in trying it again anytime soon.

I tried speed for the first time in 1983 at a track meet during my junior year of high school. I remember thinking before I put this in my mouth, am I sure I want to try this? I took it with my neighbor friend David Haselhorst. I remember David acting like a fool at the track meet and being loud and telling everyone about the speed. I distanced myself from David after that because I didn't want anyone to know what I had done and what I had tried. Taking that drug gave me an incredible feeling beyond belief. It literally made your hair feel like it was standing on end and it gave you enormous amounts of energy. Taking that pill felt like it made you invincible and there was nothing you could not do.

I had never tried any drug before in my life besides marijuana. I was extremely hesitant about trying it, but I remember telling myself, to hell with it, and went ahead and did it. It was a decision that I thought about a bit before I ingested it. These things literally made you feel incredible. Doing something illegal was exciting and exhilarating for me, too. It was about taking a walk on the wild side for me.

No one knew anything about me taking these drugs with the exception of the guy selling it to me, whom during that time I swore to secrecy. The thrill of doing something illegal was intoxicating to me, not to mention the euphoria that the drug gave me.

I knew it was wrong but I justified it in my mind at the time and then it became exciting. This became Todd's secret. And that was a whole lot of fun.

I was good, good at a lot of things. My senior year, I never lost a track meet in the high jump, setting a school record that still exists at 6-foot-8. Our track team – which consisted of only five individuals – won the state track title and I won the state championship in high jump. I was very proud of that.

I took speed for a few track meets during the season, and it definitely helped me run faster and jump higher, because it accelerated everything. I also took it before a few basketball games, but I didn't like that as much because it threw everything out of whack by going so fast. My jump shot was rushed and my timing was off, so I never did that again. Plus, I hated it because it would keep me up all night. Whenever I took speed, I could never sleep.

*** *** ***

During my high school years we would spend our time cruising down this street called Santa Fe, which was the thing to do, just driving up and down the long street and making turns at one end at the Sonic and at the other end in Kwik Stop. We often would have a 12-pack of beer in the car as we cruised Santa Fe drinking brews and trying to pick up chicks.

My first car wreck was alcohol-related, and nobody knew that until now. The neighbor kids and I were out in the country drinking beers before a Loverboy concert. On the way to the concert a man named Jack Beverly Jr., pulled out in front of me and I had to swerve to miss hitting him because he froze in my lane. I hit the telephone pole and totaled my beautiful fully-restored 1972 Chevy Nova. I was just sick over it and had I not been drinking prior to that concert, I might have reacted quicker when he pulled out in front of me and I wouldn't have been speeding. I later bought a 1976 Chevy Camaro that was canary yellow and a beautiful car.

I had a few other alcohol-related embarrassments growing up. Mary Peterson was my prom date but I had to leave her and be dropped off by my friends near the bushes by my house because I was so drunk. I woke up the next day getting arrested by the Salina police. I was misidentified by someone in a theft, and they later apologized, but nonetheless they took me down to the station to be questioned.

It was always something when I had a drink in my hand.

5

Chapter

GETTING MY FIRST TASTE
OF RECRUITING FROM COLLEGES

Recruiting was crazy my senior year in high school. I had over 200 offers from every conference in the country. Because I did so well academically, I even had Ivy League schools after me from my junior year on. The recruiting was crazy, with constant phone calls and visits to my house, as well as coaches following me everywhere.

The recruiting visits I took were wild. There was a lot of alcohol, a lot of women and more promises than I could count. I often woke up the next day in bed with a college beauty, and I had absolutely no idea where the hell I was. I have a lot of stories.

My very first recruiting visit was to Pan American University during my junior year in 1983. Lon Kruger – who's gone on to have a great 30-year college career – was the young coach then at Pan American. The highlight of that trip was going to South Padre Island and hanging out on the beach. That was their sell of the school, because nothing else was very dazzling on campus and they even put me up in a dorm for my visit. It was nothing great, that's for sure.

The next visit my junior year was to Arkansas State University. They put me up in a nasty hotel and the highlight of that visit was going to the football game. There was literally nothing more I remember about that visit. I'm not sure why I even went to visit any of these schools because I knew there was no way in hell I was going to go there. I think I went just to go somewhere. Being so poor growing up, I had never been anywhere so it was a chance for me to go somewhere and see something. That can be my only explanation for going.

I even took other recruiting visits within the state, going to small schools like Fort Hays State and Washburn. Those were incredibly fun trips, where they took me to bars and put me up in nice hotels and introduced me to pretty college girls, some of whom I often ended up hooking up with. Those trips were all about the alcohol, the fun and the women. I never had an interest in going to the schools, but I loved the visits.

Kansas State was another great visit because Tim Jankovitch, the assistant coach for K-State at the time, took me out to a local bar and I ended up hooking up with some beautiful college girl. I went to her house in the middle of nowhere. I just remember waking up in the morning and not knowing where the heck I was. As she was sleeping, I called Tim and he came to get me. I laughed about that whole experience, what a great time it was.

Those trips were my first taste of college basketball.

It tasted pretty good.

I had a lot of schools inquiring from all over the country as well. Because I was such a good student, I heard a lot from the Ivy League schools like Harvard, Yale, Cornell and Princeton.

Big, tall kids who are great students are always popular with those Ivy League schools. I never visited any of them, but it was nice to know they wanted me. It was proof that I was a good student, too.

Chapter

GETTING SPURNED BY KANSAS AND GOING TO JUNIOR COLLEGE

I had more than 200 schools recruit me in high school, some harder than others. I had plenty of offers from schools in practically every conference in the country. But the offer I wanted, I didn't get. I begged them and begged them for six months, but the offer never came.

Kansas.

The Jayhawks wanted me, but they didn't have room for me. They had four starters coming back and had already signed a few recruits, including Danny Manning, who would become a star. I wanted to stay close to home and be a part of that program. I also liked Kansas State, and they were really good at the time. But they had a numbers problem, too, and didn't offer me either. So even though I had a ton of other offers, as an 18-year-old I made a ballsy move and decided to go to junior college for a year and go Division I from there. I walked away from a bunch of free rides and wasn't real happy about, but I figured it was worth it in the long run because I wanted to go big-time and stay in Kansas.

I decided to go to Barton County Community College in Great Bend, Kansas. They were part of what was probably the best junior college league in the country – the Kansas Jayhawk Community College Conference – and I played against a lot of really

33

good players there. It was a big deal that I wound up there and I was a preseason All-American coming into my freshman year at Barton County.

My recruitment to Barton County was interesting once it looked like I was going to consider the junior college route. The Barton coaches were Jerry Mullen and Charlie Sprott, and they were really good. When Coach Mullen recruited me, he brought all his starters with him in his car to my house. That was special and I had never seen that type of recruitment before. The whole team basically came and told me they wanted me to come play with them. I liked them all right from the start.

Coach Mullen was a great coach and he was tough. He didn't play mind games, but he would always push you to get better. Coach Mullen instilled a toughness in me that I feel like I still carry with me to this day. I remember one time when I was extremely sick and running a high fever, he told me to get out there and practice and don't be a pussy. So, sicker than crap and with sweats on from head to toe, I went out and practiced with the flu to prove my toughness. I remember getting through that practice as sick as I was, and the feeling of accomplishment was incredible. I was sick but I pushed through it, both mentally and physically, and prevailed. It taught me a lot to always push through the tough times.

Going to Barton might have been one of the best experiences I had in college. Great Bend was a small community in basically the middle of nowhere. The campus was in the country on top of a large hill that overlooked everything. On a stormy day you could go outside and just watch all the tornadoes form and touch ground all around you. It was a small, little place out in the country and it had a lot of critters running around the campus all the time. We'd see foxes, coyotes, raccoons, large bull snakes and even a bunch of field mice. It was definitely small-town Kansas. Most of the athletes lived in duplexes on campus, and I spent a lot of time in the commons area playing pool and ping pong. That was about all there was to do. Other than doing that, we would just basically hang out with each other. Life was pretty mundane, just school, practice, and then a few hours of hanging out in the commons.

School was extremely easy for me academically. Sacred Heart had prepared me well for college, and I had a 4.0 grade point average at Barton. A lot of kids have to go to junior college instead of a Division I school because they can't cut it in the classroom, but that wasn't the case for me. I always liked school and always got good grades. My being there had more to do with having to wait on Kansas than anything.

I had a lot of fun there, too. Living on campus was exciting for me because it was the first time away from home for me. I reveled in the freedom. I spent my time chasing after the pretty women on campus and in town and did fairly well with the ladies. I hung out in town at a small little tavern and played pool and snooker. On the weekends, we frequented a local night club called the Chapter, where we would drink and dance the night away and hope to get lucky with a pretty lady.

The basketball was really good there. We had a great team and were considered the favorites to win the junior college national championship. Coach Mullen was a fiery character that got after us all the time. Coach Sprott was a big teddy bear who was the opposite of Coach Mullen. Coach Mullen would often scream and yell and had a constant scowl on his face that scared people. We had incredible talent on our team. Myself, Andre Harris and Maurice Smith were all Division I players, and we had a lot of other really good players, too.

At my first tournament in Midland, Texas, I made the all-tournament team and played extremely well and the crazy recruiting started all over for me again. I had a lot of colleges after me again. The Kansas and Kansas State coaches practically lived on campus at Barton, and they both wanted me really bad. The Kansas guys were always reminding me that I was supposed to come with them, so it got to be pretty weird.

We had a lot of big moments during the year. We beat Independence Junior College that year and they had Harvey Grant, who played in the NBA for a long time. They had the nation's longest home-court winning streak and we broke it. It didn't end the way we wanted it too, though. We got upset by Hutchinson Junior College early in the tournament to end our season. We were favored to win the national title and we didn't even make it to nationals. It was very disappointing, so much so that Coach Mullen decided to get out of coaching after that. I felt really bad about that.

There was a lot of buzz in the stands that night though. By then, Indiana had been recruiting me really hard. Jim Crews and Joby Wright, the two big IU assistants at the time, recruited me a lot and they had seen me play. Well, that night, IU's coach Bob Knight was in attendance to watch me play and that was a huge deal. He saw my last junior college game.

It was an interesting time with my recruiting and Coach Mullen and Coach Sprott always had my back. They knew I had begged Kansas and K-State for six months to get a scholarship offer in high school and they never came. So I started jerking them both around a little bit at Barton, and Coach Sprott thought it was pretty funny. Both KU and K-State recruiters were now after me big-time, begging me for six months to come to their school after I had begged them for six months and got nowhere. To be completely honest, when that time came to make a college decision, I basically just strung them along because I knew in my mind I was not going to go to either school, because of what they had done to me a year earlier. Coach Sprott and I laughed about it all the time because he knew what I was doing and why I was doing it. We had fun with them.

I have to admit, I had a lot of fun at Barton. My teammates were fun to be around, and we had a good time together. I often went home to Salina on the weekends – it was only like an hour and fifteen minutes away – and I would bring some of the guys with me. Coach would let me borrow his car and he had this big, huge Pontiac Bonneville. What a sight that must have been, me rolling into town in that big old Bonneville, a car full of brothers and me, the only white guy, driving this long car weighed down with all the guys.

While at Barton County, the athletes were allowed to work to make some money, which came in handy. So I worked in Coach Mullen's office, and my job every day was to do the laundry after practice. I was thankful to do that because it put a few dollars in my pocket, and money was hard to come by back then. I never got any money from my parents.

I did plenty of drinking there, and some drugs, too. I smoked weed with some of my other teammates on occasions, but I never really liked it and what it did to me. It gave me a feeling of not being in control, much like being drunk, and I didn't really like that. At Barton County was the first time I had ever seen a white powder drug called crank. I watched one of my roommates snort it regularly. I never tried it then, or even had the thought of wanting to try it.

My teammate Andre Harris smoked a lot of weed, and that would become a problem later for him. Indiana was really recruiting him hard, and they wanted both of us. We were friendly, but we really weren't friends. Andre was extremely quiet and really kept

37

to himself. He really didn't hang out too much with anyone. He loved his weed and smoked it regularly. Our relationship at Barton was pretty much that of just teammates. He came home with me a time or two to Salina to stay the weekend or have dinner, but not that often.

After the loss against Hutchinson that ended our season, Coach Knight asked me if I would come visit Indiana. I said yes, of course. I had a family ski vacation to Breckenridge planned for spring break because one of my mom's brothers owned a condo in Colorado. We stayed there for free, so I went on that trip. After I got back, I went on the visit to Indiana.

And the recruiting, the heavy recruiting, started all over again.

7

Chapter

TAKING MY COLLEGE VISITS FROM JUNIOR COLLEGE

I **had a lot of schools** that wanted me to come take visits, but I had to narrow down the list. It wasn't really all that hard. Kansas and Kansas State, of course, had to stay on the list, even though I had been having fun screwing with them. I really liked Oklahoma too, and added them to the list. Indiana was there, too. I had told Coach Knight I would come for a visit the night he came out to see me. They were a must, for sure.

The visit where I had the most fun was at Kansas State. Coach Tim Jankovitch took me out to Kite's, and I met a beautiful woman and had a great night. Kansas State really wanted me bad. They were at Barton all the time.

I never went on an official visit to Oklahoma, but I went to Norman for a track meet and got to meet one of the assistant coaches and quite a few players on that trip. It was weird, because a lot of players were telling stories about how if I signed there, I could expect a shoe box with $10,000 in cash in it and that people would hand me cash in handshakes after all the games.

Kansas' recruiting of me was interesting, too. Larry Brown was the head coach at Kansas at the time and he talked to me on the phone a lot at Barton, and his assistants were there all the time. They always talked to me like I was already theirs, since they knew

39

it was a huge deal in small-town Kansas when Indiana basketball coach Bob Knight came to recruit me at Barton. We lost, but he offered anyway.

I wanted to come there the year before, and now they were going to make that happen. I planned to take an official visit to Kansas, but I was going to visit Indiana first.

Indiana was the most laid back visit of all of them. At Indiana, I watched IU play Michigan on CBS and lost. I went out to eat with Steve Alford and Delray Brooks at Jeremiah Sweeney's and then we all went to a movie.

After the movie, I was dropped off at the student union, which was where I was staying, and at 11 p.m. while I was in bed, there was a knock at the door. Coach Knight had sent a manager to get me and take me to Assembly Hall to talk with him. After we finished our discussion, Coach and I were walking down the ramp at Assembly Hall. He put his arm around me – and it's past midnight at this point – and he says, "So son, are you coming?

Just like that, I said yes. And that was that.

To this day, I don't know why I didn't tell him I needed to think about it. I just said yes and the next thing I know, I was on IU's private plane at 7 in the morning, headed back to Kansas with the assistants to tell my parents. Remember now, back then there were no cell phones or anything for me to call them and let them know what was going on.

So, to say the least, they were very surprised and not the least bit happy. My parents and everyone else – including me, really – thought I was going to Kansas. Larry Brown, the coach at Kansas, thought I was going to Kansas, too. To this day, other than the sheer intimidation of Coach Knight, I still don't understand why I made the decision I did and how I made the decision.

It all happened so quickly.

Too quickly.

TODD JADLOW & TOM BREW

8

Chapter

TELLING THE KANSAS SCHOOLS
NO WAS VERY HARD TO DO

Telling the coaches at Kansas that I had changed my mind was probably the hardest thing I had ever done. Those guys basically lived on campus all year with me at Barton, just like the Kansas State coaches. I was seeing them practically every day.

And the Kansas coaches, of course, were convinced that I was going there all along. Their natural arrogance had them thinking that it was a done deal a year ago, that the whole plan of me going to Barton for a year and then coming to Lawrence was already etched in stone.

When I told them that I was going to Indiana, they went ballistic. I'm basically this 19-year-old kid and they are yelling and screaming at me. They said, "Do you know who you are going to play for, and do you realize what you are getting yourself into by playing for him?"

It was just a few months earlier that Coach Knight had had his infamous chair-throwing incident in that game against Purdue. It was national news, of course, and people were still talking about it. Heck, they still talk about it now, more than 30 years later.

Coach Brown and his staff at Kansas then went public in the media and told them I had reneged on my commitment to them and so forth. They had just buried me in the local media, from the

43

THE UNIVERSITY OF KANSAS
DEPARTMENT OF INTERCOLLEGIATE ATHLETICS

Allen Field House   •   Lawrence, Kansas 86045-8881

March 12, 1985

Todd Jadlow
c/o Basketball Office
Barton County Community College
BCCC Living Center
Box 57
Great Bend, KS   67530

Dear Todd,

Coach Hill informed me that you have chosen to go to school at Indiana University. I want to wish you the best of luck and am happy for you , if you have found what you want. Only you know the right decision and I will support you if you feel you have made it.

I am, however, disappointed because I truly felt we fulfilled our commitments to you. When we visited last year, you told me that you would go to junior college for a year and then would come to K.U. Your invitation was still open here and I have to feel that you knew you were a big part for our plans in the future.

Todd, I am also upset that you did not have the respect for me to let me know of your decision. You also did not visit our campus as you stated you would and I really feel cheated in that respect. You are going to make commitments in life and you are going to find out that it is important to carry through with them.

I want to wish you the best of luck in your career at Indiana. Coach Knight is truly a great coach and I know you will learn a great deal from him. Please give my regards to your family and Coach Mullen.

Sincerely,

Larry Brown
Head Basketball Coach

LB:sm

"Home of the Kansas Jayhawks"

This is the letter that Larry Brown sent me after I chose Indiana over Kansas. That's just something you don't do in recruiting. When I told the Indiana coaches about it, Coach Knight called Brown and ripped him.

Kansas City Star to the Lawrence Journal That's just not something that's done in the recruiting game. He even sent me a nasty letter, which is never done.

Here's the gist of what he said:

"I am, however, disappointed because I truly felt we fulfilled our commitments to you. When we visited last year, you told me that you would go to junior college for a year and then come to K.U. Your invitation was still open here and I have to feel that you knew you were a big part of our plans in the future.

"Todd, I am also upset that you did not have the respect for me to let me know of your decision. You also did not visit our campus as you stated you would and I really feel cheated in that respect. You are going to make commitments in life and you are going to find out that it is important to carry through with them."

I remember speaking with the coaches at Indiana about it, and they weren't happy. Coach Knight and Coach Brown weren't necessarily the best of friends, but they had both been around a while and knew each other well enough. Coach Knight apparently called Coach Brown and went off on him for taking this issue public. I had heard later that he really blistered him.

What can I say? I thought I was going to Kansas too, but I just changed my mind. It happens. Nonetheless, Coach Brown was angry and let it be known in the media. It was classless.

In retrospect, the fact that Coach Brown acted that way shouldn't have been all that surprising. He's a snake, always has been and always will be. He's been in trouble with the NCAA at just about every stop he's made. And if you tell him no, he gets really angry.

I still can't believe that he actually had to audacity to write me a letter to complain about my decision. I've kept that letter for 30 years, and I still shake my head in amazement that he had the gall to write it in the first place. And I still laugh that he felt I cheated him. That's funny coming from a guy who's been caught cheating by the NCAA at every school he's been at.

There have been many times that I've questioned my decision to go to Indiana, but I would have questioned my decision to go to Kansas just as much, I'm sure.

When it was all said and done with my recruiting, in the end I was an Indiana Hoosier.

9

Chapter

1986 AT INDIANA, MY
SEASON ON THE BRINK

When you spend four years playing basketball for Bob Knight at Indiana, there are about a thousand moments that come up that make you wonder why the hell you're there. That was certainly the case for me, and I'm sure every one of my fellow IU players would concur that it's happened to them, too.

It didn't take me long at all to question my decision to go to Indiana. Before my first season at Indiana had even started in 1985-86, I thought I had made a huge mistake.

A lot of things played into that. It was hard to be so far away from home, and what made that worse was my dad was dealing with a cancer issue and it was difficult to not be around to see him. He had testicular cancer and it had spread to his lymph nodes and he needed surgery. I hated not being able to be there. I was already homesick, and that made it that much harder, being so far away.

That first year at Indiana was pure hell, and most avid college basketball fans know all about that year because that was the season that the great writer John Feinstein spent several months embedded in our program. Coach Knight had given him unprecedented access to him and the program, and Feinstein wrote the

IU Archives P0059082

Coach Knight and I had a lot of conversations along the sidelines during my Indiana games. Some were more civil than others.

book "Season On The Brink," about that season. I'm in there, a
little bit.

Feinstein came to Bloomington because Coach Knight was
the most high-profile, controversial coach in college basketball. He
had already won national championships in 1976 and 1981 and he
coached the 1984 U.S. Olympic Team to a gold medal. But he was
starting to melt down a bit, and it all came to a head in the spring
of 1985 when he threw that chair across the court in a game against
Purdue. The video of the chair-toss has probably been viewed
50-million times. Feinstein thought it would be great to spend a
year with him, and really show what kind of guy he was. Everyone
was shocked when Coach said yes.

Feinstein was around all the time and everything he wrote
in that book is 100 percent truthful and accurate. Coach Knight
was brutal on us from the day we all showed up on campus, because he was adamant about not putting up with another season
like the last one. I had just gotten there, and had nothing to do with
the 1985 season, but it didn't matter. He was brutal on everybody,
including me. From the minute I got there, he was always yelling
and screaming, mostly about how he would not put up with another
year like 1985 had been. It seemed like every sentence of his
started with "You motherf------." He was relentless.

I felt like I had made a huge mistake.

I wasn't alone either. When I had come for my official visit
the previous spring, I spent most of my time with Steve Alford and
Delray Brooks. Steve was the All-American boy who had already
had two great seasons at Indiana and was even part of Coach
Knight's Olympic team with Michael Jordan and Patrick Ewing.
Steve might be the most popular Indiana player ever.

Delray was also a Mr. Basketball from Indiana, and when
he came to Bloomington from Michigan City, it was a big deal,

49

too. But Delray, who was my next-door neighbor at the Jackson Heights apartment complex that we all lived in, just never fit in at Indiana. Delray was so bad at Indiana because Coach had just eaten his confidence alive. We talked about how unhappy he was all the time. Delray had lost everything. He hated Coach Knight and he hated being at Indiana. I mean, it was really sad how beaten down – and broken down – Delray was.

Delray wanted to transfer and Coach Knight had no problem with him leaving. Hell, he was practically begging him to leave every single day. At the time, Rick Pitino, who has won national championships at Kentucky and Louisville, was coaching at Providence and Delray had talked to him about transferring there.

What no one knew until right now is that Delray and I talked about transferring there together. He had talked to Coach Pitino about me several times and the door was open for me to transfer to Providence as well. I had only been in Bloomington for a few months and I was ready to leave. I called my parents and told them that I wanted to transfer, but they would have nothing of it. They both told me that I had started at Indiana and I was going to finish at Indiana. We talked for hours about it and they told me I needed to stick it out. So I did, but I really didn't want to.

There were several things that made me want to leave. I was already beaten down, both physically and mentally, before I had even played my first game. There was no way I was physically ready for Big Ten basketball at Indiana, but even worse I wasn't ready for all the mental mind games. There was so much going on in my head that I couldn't keep up with it all.

***   ***   ***

My first year at IU, I was certainly not prepared for

playing for Coach Knight. During this time, he was going through a divorce with his first wife Nancy and I believe he often brought his anger and troubles from his marriage into our practices. So many days were filled rage and violent outbursts, which were all chronicled in "Season on the Brink." Every player truly says and thinks they can handle anything thrown at them and I thought my junior college coach, Jerry Mullen, was a tough SOB. I thought I was prepared to play under Coach Knight after playing for Coach Mullen. How completely wrong I was. Coach Mullen was a pussy-cat compared to Coach Knight.

What made is so tough? First, the physical.

Right after school started in August, the preseason work-outs started, too, and what a world that is as a freshman coming into a major Division 1 program. You start out with a two-mile run from Assembly Hall down fraternity row and then to the track, where trainer Tim Garl, who's still at Indiana, took you through the grueling workouts. After the two-mile run, we'd do 10 timed 220-yard dashes followed by 10 timed 100-yard dashes, followed by 10 timed 40-yard dashes. If everyone doesn't make the time, then that run does not count, so it's a team concept as well, right from the beginning. After the track dashes, we'd go do stadium hops, maybe four stadium hops from the bottom of the stadium to the top. After all that, you walk over to Assembly Hall and get changed for on-court workouts or scrimmages for about an hour and a half. Then you head down to the weight room for another hour to an hour and a half of weight training. This would be a typical day for a pre-season workout. It would practically kill you. Every day.

You would think that when the first day of practice starts you would have good legs and a base from the months of pre-season workouts, but it is truly like you have never done anything. The practices were so grueling and hard that the next day you

Andre Harris (34) was my teammate at Barton and came with me to Indiana, but we weren't really that close. He was in trouble all the time at IU.

would have severe blisters on your feet and your muscles hurt in a way that I couldn't even describe. You can barely walk, they are that hard.

And the mental? It was everything, right on down to being ripped for being a bad roommate.

Because we played at Barton together, they roomed me with Andre Harris when I got there and that was somewhat weird and difficult. Dre was a nice guy, but he was an extreme introvert. I consider myself introverted as well, but not to that degree. Andre was something of an invisible figure, very private, a man of few words and very difficult to read and understand.

To say he had a hard time at IU would be an understatement. He didn't like to go to class and when he didn't go, guess who got chewed out for it? I did. I couldn't believe it the first time he missed class and I got called into the coaches office and got my ass handed to me for not taking him to class. Like that was my job. I told them I took him every chance I could. But Andre, unbeknownst to me, was telling the coaching staff that I would just leave him at the apartment. So the coaches literally chewed my ass off and blamed me for Andre not going to class. After that meeting, I made a conscious effort every day to get Andre up and to take him to class. I literally became his bitch or taxi. Numerous times I would knock on Andre's door and say, "Andre, are you ready to go to class?" and his typical answer would be "No, I will just catch up with you later."

Well, not long after that, I got called into the coaches' offices again and asked what was going on with Andre not going to class. I told them I can only do so much and that every time I ask him to go, he says no. The coaches finally moved Andre out of our apartment and into a dorm on campus. But I felt the coaches held these ill feelings against me because Andre was lying to them.

Especially Joby Wright, he came down hard on me. Here I was, trying to get settled myself, and they were taking it out on me for what Andre was doing.

Nothing changed after Andre moved into the dorm. He still missed class and near the end of the year he failed a drug test for marijuana and they kicked him off the team. It was somewhat a vindication for me and what I had be telling them all along, but not a single coach ever apologized to me for all the shit they said and put me through by accusing me of not taking care of him.

I'll say this about Andre. He was the only player I ever saw try to stand up against Coach Knight when he was getting yelled at. When Coach Knight gets to that stage of angry, you know it's a scary thing. But Andre Harris snapped right back at him one day and I thought oh, my God, this isn't going to go well.

A lot of times in practice, Coach would point out things while we were playing and practicing and sometimes he would be 100 percent wrong, but he would get after you anyway, just to see your reaction. And if you don't take it like a man, well, then he'd make it even worse.

Let's say, for example, a guy cuts across the lane and you switch men and somebody scores on me. It's not your man anymore, because that's our defensive plan. But Coach will come after you and say, "God damn, it's your man." And you know it's not your man, because our defense was said to switch. But Coach, he still comes out to you and gets in your face and basically spits on you. I was young and so was Andre, but he just basically stood up to him and got right in Coach's face and said it wasn't his man. He's telling Coach that he doesn't know what he's talking about. I thought World War Three was going to start.

Coach is just yelling and screaming and circling around him, right up into him. I had never seen anything like that before. I think if he could have killed Andre that day, he would have.

Seeing Coach go nuts happened all the time. Most every day, prior to the season and throughout it, Coach Knight mentally beats you down until he owns your soul and mind and you are truly just a puppet and he becomes the puppet master. All those years he coached, why do you think so many players looked over at him on the bench after they screwed up in a game? Why? Because you are going through things in your mind all the time when you're out there instead of just playing.

When you first get there, you are constantly afraid of making a mistake of any kind. Instead of just truly concentrating on the game and being so mentally focused in the game you tend to worry about him and his reactions after a bad play. Call it maturity or what, but I constantly was watching over my shoulder. That year truly was not fun and I often asked myself what the hell did I get into here playing for him. I wanted out in the worst way and wanted to transfer, but my parents stepped in.

A player coming to IU knows about Coach Knight and says they can handle him and anything he throws at us. That year left me wondering what the hell I got myself in to. It was straight up hell and to date maybe the hardest thing I have ever gone through in my life.

This includes me being incarcerated as well. That's how hard that year was.

*** ***** ***

Of course, being a basketball player at Indiana isn't all bad. I did have my share of fun away from the court. Several of us all lived in the same apartment complex, and it was a parade of

Daryl Thomas was a really good player and teammate with me at Indiana, and no one took more abuse -- verbal or physical -- than he did.

beautiful women in and out of our apartments. Some of us were single, others had girlfriends either on campus or back home. Still, it was a nice parade. When you were a basketball player at Indiana, lots of girls wanted to be with you, even if you already had a girlfriend. And trust me, there were lots of pretty girls in Bloomington, and I'm sure that's still true today.

Steve Alford and I were friends, or at least I thought we were. Steve had a high school sweetheart, Tanya, who's still his wife today. But he was always asking girls who were with me, "Why are you dating Todd?" I got the feeling Steve liked busting chops a little bit.

I made quite a few other good friends outside of basketball. Eric Moore, who had played football for IU at one time, introduced me to many of the football players whom I became good friends with over the years. It was one of the football guys who also got me to use steroids for the first time. Kevin Allen, who was a first-round pick of the Philadelphia Eagles, went to his doctor and got me a bottle of Anavar and Anadrol. He gave me a two month's supply of it and it literally changed my physique over the summer. I went from a skinny kid of 205 pounds to a man of 235 pounds over a two-month period in the summer. It was the first time in my life I had ever tried PED's and the feeling it gave you during the time you were on it was that of invincibility and that of great strength. It put some weight on my skinny frame.

At that time in the 80's, a lot of guys on the football team were juicing. A couple other football players I became good friends with were Pete Stoyanovich and Dan Strysinski, both whom went on to have great pro careers in the NFL. Eric introduced me to endless amounts of women my first year in college. I was always at the football house and I was probably better friends with a lot of the football guys than I was with my own basketball teammates.

57

There was a woman the football guys nicknamed "The Pizza Lady," because she always delivered. Crazy things went on when they brought recruits to the football house. I personally watched as the football recruits lined up to take turns having sex with the pizza women. At the time, under Coach Bill Mallory, it was the best recruiting tool that Indiana had. To me it was totally disgusting, but the football players and recruits absolutely loved it and the crazy things that went on in that bedroom are beyond description.

The fringe benefits of being a player at IU were limited compared to other big time programs because of the fear of God that Coach Knight put into everyone around the program. There used to be a gas station where we used to go for some free gas and get your car worked on without paying. I am not sure how it happened, but Coach Knight found out and he put the living fear of God into that owner of the filling station because one day when we went back there, the owner ran us off as quickly as we pulled in.

Occasionally we would get a free meal or two at places but it seemed that Coach Knight would always find out and would put an end to it. The same with going to a bar or club during the season, which was an unwritten no-no. If someone did go, always without fail the owner of the establishment or night club would call the basketball office and inform Coach that his players were in there. When that happened, the next practice was pure hell for everyone, so the players than basically policed the actions of everyone to insure this did not happen.

It was the same with going to class. You could be in an auditorium with over a thousand students in the class and the teacher at the start of the class would make an announcement, "Would my IU basketball players please stand up" and if you weren't there at the class, the teacher would call the basketball office to inform

Coach and all hell would break loose at practice. If one player skipped a class, everyone paid for it.

And we paid often. Coach was so pissed at us that on New Year's Eve and New Year's Day, we practically practiced 24 hours in a row. There were a few breaks in there, but it was basically nonstop. And when our season ended with a first-round loss to Cleveland State, Coach Knight went ballistic on the plane ride home. He was basically trying to tear up the plane. He was punching the windows and punching the panels on the plane.

I was truly happy when the season ended after we lost against Cleveland State. That game was horrible for us. I mean, we were confident going into that game, but nothing about that game went right. We didn't play well and it was embarrassing.

So was the plane ride home. Coach hit Daryl Thomas and grabbed him by the neck and started shaking him. He was screaming like crazy, and pounding on the walls of the plane and the windows. I thought for sure they were going to shatter. You talk about putting the fear of God in you. He was totally out of control and even the assistant coaches didn't know what to do about it. Their faces were drained white.

It was really scary just witnessing someone going nuts like that.

*** *** ***

No one got treated worse than Daryl Thomas that whole year. Daryl was a really good player, but he drove Coach nuts and he was unmerciful a lot of times to Daryl. Coach just didn't think Daryl was tough enough and he'd call him a 'f----- pussy" all the time.

One time we came into the locker room and there was a

collage of those pussies, all cut out of Penthouse magazine. Coach made the managers do it, which had to be terrible for those guys. It covered Daryl's entire locker, plastered from top to bottom. I sat next to Daryl and it literally brought him to tears and it tore me up inside to see him in this type of pain as he slowly started taking down these centerfolds. Coach saw him start to take it down, and he's yelling at Daryl, "You're not taking that down, you pussy" and "Don't touch that, you pussy."

As bad as that was, it was even worse when he played us off each other. One time, there were a lot of coaches watching practice and Coach called Steve Alford over. He said. "Steve, tell them what Daryl's nickname is."

Steve hesitated at first and didn't say anything. Then Coach asked him again and Steve said "Pussy."

I lost a little bit of respect for Steve that day. He kissed Coach's ass instead of sticking up for a teammate. That was completely disrespectful, I thought, but it's also how Coach did it. It wasn't really fair to Steve for Coach to put him in that situation.

I had some success my first year at IU. At Michigan on a CBS nationally televised game, I did do a good job guarding Roy Tarpley and scoring and was awarded the CBS Player of the Game for my efforts. I got a nice certificate for that performance.

After the Cleveland State loss, when I got back to Bloomington, I jumped in a car with Scott Eads and a friend of his and we drove from Bloomington to Daytona Beach, Florida for spring break. That would be the first and only spring break I went on because I got in a ton of trouble for going. I guess the coaches wanted me to stick around Bloomington and sulk about the loss.

I didn't. I wanted to have some fun because the basketball season certainly wasn't fun. A nightmare was an apt description.

10

Chapter

REDSHIRTING THROUGH
A NATIONAL CHAMPIONSHIP SEASON

The summer after that first year at Indiana, I was having all sorts of trouble with my ankle and it required surgery. It was going to require a good bit of rehab and the coaches wanted to redshirt me, which I thought was a good thing at the time because I didn't want to waste a year if I wasn't going to be healthy.

It wasn't a little thing, because my ankle was a mess and surgery was pretty much mandatory. I had a lot of talks about it with Coach Knight and the trainers and doctors, and we all agreed it was the right thing to do. It was a good three months of rehab and I really didn't feel myself again until the season was about to start. We decided on the redshirt right after surgery.

But the down side of it was that we were going to have a really good team. Steve Alford was back for his senior year and he was already an All-American. Daryl Thomas, for all the grief he took from Coach, was back too, and he was a really good player. Ricky Calloway was a young kid ready to burst on the scene and Coach Knight had recruited a couple more junior college players, Dean Garrett and Keith Smart, and everyone could tell right away that they were going to be able to help us.

The hardest part about redshirting is that once you feel better, you do everything that everyone else does, expect for play

IU Archives P0044677

Steve Alford was the star and the leader of our 1987 national championship team. He was a great shooter and a real fan favorite.

in the games. That was hard. So my contribution to the team was to practice hard against the starters every day and help make them better. I basically played against Dean Garrett every day in practice and I did what I could to help him get better.

That season was so different from my first year there. Coach Knight is a completely different person when you're winning and playing well, and we really did that year. The players, we all called that a "country club" year because that's what it was like. It seemed like Coach was always in a good mood, which was the complete opposite from the year before when he was always pissed off and yelling at us.

It was pretty obvious early on that this was going to be a big year for us and the talk of winning it all started pretty early, too. The fan base was totally on board, and they were nuts at every game.

This was all new to me. I have to be totally honest when I say that I didn't know anything about the history of Indiana basketball when I got there. When they started recruiting me, all I knew was that they had a coach who screamed a lot. I didn't know about the other national championships or all that history of basketball in Indiana that goes back forever.

I didn't even know how many national championship Indiana had won until I got to Bloomington for the first time and saw the championship banners inside Assembly Hall. When I was growing up, I never watched college basketball on TV or anything. Growing up in Salina, I might pay attention to Kansas or Kansas State a little, but I didn't even do much of that, to be honest. I kind of went from sport to sport as a kid, but I was much more about playing them than watching them. It's not like now, where everybody has access to all the stats and the records and everything. I never read anything like that as a kid.

Keith Smart came to Indiana out of junior college and he really helped us have a great year. He hit the game-winner in the NCAA title game.

***   ***   ***

Being one of the older guys now, I got a chance to entertain recruits a little bit. I was still living in Jackson Heights apartments, and we still had a lot of fun. The most memorable recruit that I took care of who stayed at my apartment during his visit was this kid from Concord, Indiana named Shawn Kemp. He was a junior in high school then, but everyone already knew he was going to be a star and Coach Knight really wanted him.

I took care of him on his visit and took him to a couple of parties in the Jackson Heights complex, introduced him to a few girls and I think he had a really good time. He got to see first-hand the social scene at Indiana and what it was like to be an IU basketball player. Shawn wound up signing with Kentucky but he never played there. He was a horrible student and couldn't get a high enough SAT score to be eligible. He left after a few months and transferred to a junior college and then turned pro. He played 14 years in the NBA but it's funny that he quickly forgot about all the little people. My rookie year in the NBA with the New Jersey Nets, we were playing in the summer league and I had to play against Shawn, who was the first-round pick of the Seattle SuperSonics. I lined up against him the whole game and he didn't even recognize me or say one word to me about taking care of him at Indiana. I guess in his mind he was too big-time to talk to me, or even say "What's up, Todd?" Not a word or peep from him. I guess he had a pretty short-term memory.

***   ***   ***

I remember that even though I couldn't play in the games, that I had a terrific year practicing every day against Dean

65

Garrett. I believe I did a heck of a job getting him ready for the year. He really improved a lot over the course of the year and he helped us win a lot of games. I take a lot of pride in playing a role in that.

That's the strange thing about being a redshirt. You do everything all the other players do, except you just don't get to play in the games. Every practice, you're there. Every film session, you're there. Every meal, every meeting, everything. I didn't go on the road with the team, but when they came back, you were expected to be there when they got back. I would watch the games on TV and then I would call one of the managers and find out what time the guys would be getting back. Even when it was the middle of the night, you were expected to be there. I never missed, because I didn't want to find out what the repercussions would be.

Coach Knight actually treated me pretty well that year. He'd bark now and then at practice, but not very often and never for too long. That '87 season was night and day from the year before. When things are going well, Coach is completely different. Sure, we were really good that year, but we played that way and, even more importantly, we practiced that way all the time, too. We did what Coach wanted, we had experienced guys like Steve and Daryl, and Dean Garrett and Keith Smart fit right in as the new junior college guys.

My ankles felt pretty good and I was able to practice hard all year long. I gave Dean and Daryl all I could in practice every day and I think I helped them. Brian Sloan and Steve Eyl played up front too, and they were shorter than I was but they could play. That's part of the reason they figured they could redshirt me, but there were times I think Coach had wished I would have been available. More than a few times at practice, when he was pissed at Daryl or some of the other big guys were struggling, he'd go off on them and use me to do it. "Goddammit, if we had Jadlow, we might be a decent team," he'd say. There were a few games too, where the matchups weren't great, and some of the coaches told me they wished I could have played in those games.

It was tough missing the games, but it was such a fun year that I really didn't mind it. Mostly it was nice to just not get yelled at all the time.

Coach was still tough on Daryl Thomas a lot of that year, but Daryl brought some of that on himself too. Daryl didn't like always going to class, and whenever he skipped a class, Coach always knew about it right away. And we all paid for it in practice.

It's one thing if you are getting A's and B's, and occasionally miss a class for something. Nothing ever got said about that. But if your grades weren't good or you were doing it all the time, then we all had to deal with it. I can't tell you how many times Coach would walk into practice and he'd call a player out for not going to class and then we'd all start running. You just knew that was going to be a bad, bad day. That year, when it happened, it was usually because of Daryl.

***   ***   ***

We really played well all season that year. We won 14 out of our first 15 games, with the only loss at Vanderbilt in December. That was right after the Kentucky game, so that's no excuse or anything, but we had put a lot into the Kentucky game, and with good reason.

Actually, it was only one reason. Coach just hated Kentucky, and he hated them with a passion. So winning that game was critical, especially after what had happened a year earlier.

Coach hated Kentucky more than any other school we

67

played against, even Purdue. The year before, Steve got suspended for a game for appearing in a charity calendar, and it was the Kentucky game that he had to miss. The irony of it all wasn't lost on Coach. There was no doubt in Coach's mind that Kentucky was cheating like crazy and at Indiana, he ran a really clean program. So Steve poses for this calendar, which some sorority was doing to raise money for a good cause, some good charity.

In public, Coach ripped the NCAA and ripped Kentucky and how much the whole thing was a joke. In public, Coach defended Steve, but behind closed doors he really laid in to Steve for not checking to see if it was OK to do it in the first place. So when we lost down there without Steve, man that just burned Coach up.

So the Kentucky game was one game that was a must win. It was funny, because Coach used to call us mother f------ all the time, but with Kentucky, he was always saying "Those mother

IU Archives P0059111
My job in 1987 as a redshirt was to come to practice every day and play hard. I did that, and Coach Knight has always told me he appreciated that.

f------ this" or "Those mother f------ that." That was the only week Coach didn't call us mother f------. Coach knew Kentucky was cheating and they got caught right after that too. There were a lot of dollars floating around down there from all those horse people and Coach knew it. We beat them, and it was a good thing we did.

We won the Big Ten and only lost four regular-season games all year. We lost to Iowa when they were No. 1 in the country – we were No. 3 at the time – and they were really good. We beat them later in Bloomington. We lost a couple games late to Purdue and Illinois, but when the NCAA Tournament rolled around, we were a No. 1 seed and confident we could make some noise.

Traveling for the NCAA Tournament games was a great experience for me, especially since my only experience with it the year before was so horrible with that loss to Cleveland State. It was really nice to be a part of the championship run. We played our first two games in Indianapolis and won easily, then we went to Cincinnati for the regionals and we beat LSU and Duke there. I often tell everyone to win the NCAA tournament it takes a good team, a team playing well at the right time, and a little bit of luck to advance and win in this tournament. This year we had all of the above.

We went to New Orleans for the Final Four and that was a blast. There were Indiana fans everywhere and everyone had lots of friends and family around too. Even my parents came. You know, it's funny when you see Final Fours in New Orleans, you'll see teams there three or four days early and players out on Bourbon Street and all that, but that wasn't us. It was another business trip for us and everything was still very regimented. Obviously we weren't allowed to leave the hotel. Everything is regimented, just like it always was. We didn't deviate from anything. And we were going to keep doing it, which I understood and agreed with.

We beat UNLV in a classic game in the semifinals and then we played Syracuse for the championship. Steve was incredible that night, but it was Keith Smart who became famous for hitting the game-winning shot over in the corner that still gets replayed every March. It was amazing just enjoying it all. It was Coach's third national championship in 11 years, but it was a first for all of us and we really enjoyed it. The celebration in the locker room was great.

I remember Coach coming over to me in the locker room and putting his arm around me. I think he wanted to make sure I didn't feel left out, and I didn't. He told me to cherish this, even though I didn't get to play on this team. He kept saying "Next year, we're really going to need you." He kept calling me his "Kansas Tornado." It was a fun night.

Afterward, we walked around to each other's rooms and talked in the hotel. Some of us eventually went out to Bourbon Street and hung out until about three in the morning. We hung out with some fans but we couldn't be drinking or anything. Most of us weren't old enough and we wouldn't do that anyway. It was just fun to be out because that's something we would never get to do. Road trips, we never left the hotel, so this was different.

Most people, honestly, just stayed in the hotel. A lot of guys just hung out with their families, too. Steve had a ton of family and friends there. It was a great night, even though I didn't get to play.

So we win the championship and our trainer, Tim Garl, gives everybody a hundred bucks for our per diem. And Coach Knight says, "Tonight, and tonight only, here's the deal. The bus leaves at 7 a.m., and be on it. You'll be on the bus at 7, or you find your own way back to Bloomington." That was the only rule – be on the bus at 7.

So we're on the bus and it's getting to be 7 o'clock and we look out the window and Dan Dakich and Murry Bartow are running toward the bus, about 30 seconds late. Coach tells the bus driver to close the door and let's get out of here. Dan is knocking on the door as the bus pulls away and then he starts chasing after it and his bag comes open and his clothes are flying everywhere. Then he falls flat on his butt on the cobblestone and just throws his hands up in air as the bus pulled away. I still remember that look of despair on Dan's face. It was priceless.

That's Coach, and rules are rules. The funny thing was they took a cab to the airport and even beat us there. Coach still wouldn't let them on our plane. They had to fly back on a different plane with the media.

When we came back to Bloomington, the party never ended.

Considering that's Indiana's last NCAA championship even 30 years later, I guess that celebration is still going on for lots of people.

***   ***   ***

I **was really happy** for a lot of my teammates. Steve Alford was the leader of our team in 1987 and he was a cult figure in Indiana. He was a coach's son who had an amazing career at New Castle High School and his first three years at Indiana had been incredible. He was already a legend before I even got to Bloomington. Winning this title seemed to be something he was born to do.

My relationship with Steve wasn't much different than it was with the other players. Obviously, Steve was in charge, and rightfully so. When he was a freshman, he was immediately the

71

IN THEIR OWN WORDS

Steve Alford, Indiana (1983-87)

During our championship season in 1987, we all had defined roles. Todd's role, as a redshirt that year, was to work hard in practice to make our bigs better and he did exactly that.

Those guys like Dean Garrett and Daryl Thomas and the others had their hands full with Todd every day in practice. What always impressed me about Todd that year what that he brought it to practice every single day. And he was a lot to handle for those guys. He could run and he could shoot and he didn't mind mixing it up under the boards. Definitely, Todd showed up every day.

That was a special time for all of us. That was my senior year and for us seniors, we hadn't won a Big Ten title yet and no four-year player under Coach (Knight) had ever not won one. We won a lot of games that year, we never lost at home and we won that Big Ten title. And it was a special run through the NCAA Tournament.

Having won the Big Ten and playing close to home in Indianapolis and Cincinnati, there was less pressure on us, I think. We had a really good team and everybody played well that whole tournament. It was a lot of fun. It's hard to believe it's been 30 years already. We'll never forget it, that's for sure. And Todd always needs to feel like he was a big part of that, because he definitely was.

Steve Alford is currently the head basketball coach at UCLA.

best player on the team. In the NCAA Tournament that year, Indiana beat North Carolina in the regional semifinals and that was Michael Jordan's last college game. Carolina was No. 1 in the country and that was the game where our assistant coach Dan Dakich had become a legend for shutting down Jordan, but it was Steve who scored the most points and made all the biggest shots when it mattered. Then during the summer, Steve was selected to play on Coach Knight's U.S. Olympic team that won the gold medal and there was a lot of controversy around Coach picking him. Steve justified it though by playing great during that tournament.

I had a lot of respect for Steve, especially on the court. He was a great player and a great shooter, but he also worked very hard and helped his teammates out a lot. His play spoke for itself. My only issues with Steve were outside the court. Everybody thought they knew who he was. His image wasn't always reality. He was an incredible player but off the court he'd say some things that made me mad, especially about girls I'd be seeing. He could bust your chops. A lot of us lived together and close to each other at Jackson Heights apartments and believe me, there were women coming and going from those apartments all the time.

Steve had a high school sweetheart, Tanya, and we all knew it. But that didn't stop girls from wanting to come over to Steve's apartment all the time. I mean, they all idolized Steve. I was no angel. I slept with a lot of women that year, too, but I didn't have a girlfriend back at home. That's probably why Steve would give me grief about it, and say bad things about me to the girls I was seeing. Steve Eyl also lived at Jackson Heights, and so did Todd Meier, Brian Sloan and Jeff Oliphant. We all had our share of fun, that's for sure.

What made me mad about Steve was that he knew some of these girls I went out with and he would ask them, "Why are you going out with Todd? He's not the kind of guy you want to go out with." I asked him about it one time and he looked me right in the eye and denied it, but a couple different girls told me he said something to them. That was just Steve being sarcastic, I'm sure. Boys being boys and busting balls maybe. It was fine.

He was a heck of a teammate and a heck of a player. But behind the scenes, he didn't have the same persona as what everybody saw in public. He was just one of us guys, enjoying the benefits of being an IU basketball player. I'm really glad he's had such a great coaching career. At his five stops, he's won 527 games already and he's coaching at UCLA now, which is about as big as it gets.

That's a great career, too. He's had them both, as a player and a coach. I wish I would have spent more time with Steve after Indiana. That's a regret, for sure.

*** *** ***

I **was really happy** for Daryl Thomas when we won that title because I hoped that it made it all worthwhile, his time at Indiana and all the abuse he took from Coach.

No one should have ever had to go through that whole pussy centerfold and be called out by Coach as much as he was. I sat right next to Daryl in the locker room and I saw it all up close. I felt for him a lot of days, I really did. He was a good player – and he had a great game in the championship game against Syracuse, which really made me happy. But he's even a better person, and a super nice guy.

He's pretty much always been on everybody's list as that guy who was treated the worst by Coach. Nobody can ever come up with anybody any worse than he treated him. I mean it. Daryl brought some of it on himself. It seems like every time Daryl missed a class, Coach knew about it right away. There was a time in the preseason where Daryl just disappeared and nobody knew where he was. He didn't come to practice. That was a problem, and when he came back we all paid for that too. But he put up with a lot. Coach would throw tampons at him and put tampons in his locker and call him a pussy to his face all the time. I guess that was a great way to go out, winning.

Chapter

1988, THE LONG
YEAR AFTER THE TITLE

There were so many ups and downs my 1988 year at Indiana that it was just amazing. A lot of people thought we were going to really be good that year – me included – but that season fell apart in a hurry and it turned out to be horrible. That was really disappointing for me. We lost a lot of games and were a middle-of-the-pack Big Ten team.

And we were miserable.

It's one thing when Coach Knight is miserable and takes it all out on the players. Well, he got pretty miserable fairly early in the season in 1988, but what was different from 1986 was that the players didn't really stick together through it like we did in '86. There was a lot of divisiveness that year and it definitely caused a problem. It had a bearing on how we played, on how we practiced and even on how we just spent our year together. And it wasn't pretty, which was too bad.

A lot of it had to do with Ricky Calloway. Ricky was a good player and all, but he could cause some problems. He caused a lot of turmoil and dissention, so much so that when Coach Knight came to talk to us about him leaving the program, we were all fine with it. It takes a lot for that to happen at Indiana, to get kicked out especially if you're a good player.

77

IU Archives P0059110

Dean Garrett and I finally got a chance to play together in the 1987-88 season, but it didn't turn out how either one of us wanted.

When you talk to Coach Knight's players during his 30 years at Indiana, the issue of race almost never comes up. Through all those years, black players and white players always got along and always did things together and hung out together a lot. That wasn't the case in 1988 and it was Ricky Calloway that created the divide.

Let's back-track a little. Coming into the season, people thought we had the chance to be pretty good. Dean Garrett and Keith Smart, the junior college stars who helped us win a title the year before, were back and I was ready to play again too after getting redshirted. Ricky was a starter, Joe Hillman was back and we had two great freshman – Jay Edwards and Lyndon Jones – who were coming in from Marion High School and they were something of high school legends like Steve Alford had been because they had won three straight state championships, which is a pretty big deal in Indiana. We were preseason No. 6 in the Associated Press poll.

We were coming off a national championship, too, so that major buzz was still around campus. We used to joke all the time that it seemed like all 30,000 kids on campus walked around with national championship T-shirts on every day.

It was the same for us. The night we won the title, we got championship rings from the NCAA. They had two sets of rings made up, one gold and one silver, and they gave them to us after the game. We got the gold ones, of course, and Syracuse's players got the silver. But when we got back to Indiana, Coach had them make up nicer rings for us and that became one of my most prized possessions. It still is. It's nothing fancy or gaudy, but it's nice. I've seen some other rings and it was nothing like those Nebraska football players got, but it was still nice. And there was always this buzz on campus too, just whenever people saw you.

79

It was a good time to be an Indiana basketball player.

And it was good for me to just be a player again after redshirting in 1987. It was nice to be back out there and being ready to contribute. I took my redshirt season as a year for me to get better and I felt like I did that. It helped me learn how to play inside, which was important because I had never really been an inside player, even though I was tall. I always ran the floor in high school and junior college and I played on the perimeter as much as I went inside. So that year helped me. That year helped me grow up and mature a lot too, because I was able to better understand what Coach Knight wanted. I got more comfortable around Bloomington and around the program because there was no pressure on me as a redshirt.

Because Keith and Dean were back and they were starters the previous year, I think Coach was really counting on them to be leaders on the '88 team, but it really didn't turn out that way. Neither one of them were really very vocal, especially Keith, and it never worked out that way. Now, don't get me wrong. I'm really not saying anything bad about those two because I really like Keith and Dean, and they are great guys. But when problems cropped up that year, neither one of them were going to be that vocal team leader who kept everyone in line. They just let things happen, and it wound up ripping the team apart. It wasn't like the first two years when Steve Alford was around and he was the clear leader of the team.

The problems started and ended with Ricky, really. There would be times where he'd call out Steve Eyl, Joe Hillman, Brian Sloan and me as the white guys. He said "you guys" all the time when referring to us, and he never even wanted to have anything to do with us. So then at team meals in the Union, all the black guys starting sitting together and all the white guys sat together. Coach

80

found out that when we ate, it was one table with all the black players and another table with all the white players and Coach went ballistic. He said if he ever heard of this again he would run our asses until we couldn't walk. He got very verbal and aggressive and it might have been as mad as I've ever seen him. So from that day on, we split up but I remember Ricky not handling that well at all. He was pissed about having to sit with us.

So from that day on, we made sure that whenever we were together as a team it was mixed at every table with blacks and whites. Coach would not put up with any behavior of segregation. I truly don't think it was on purpose that our tables were like that but I could be wrong. I think it all got started with Ricky, and him wanting to be around all the black players all the time. He just didn't want to be around the rest of us. That was the kind of person he was.

What was also different about that team was that we didn't spend much time with each other away from the court. Everybody just sort of did their own thing. Brian Sloan, Steve Eyl and I would spend time together, but there wasn't much outside of that. Part of it is when things start going bad and Coach starts getting hard on you, that when it's over you just want to get away from it. We saw each other so much during the day that, honestly, when it was time to go home, you just didn't want to see anybody any more.

***　　***　　***

I joined a fraternity that year, which kept me from losing it during the trying season. I became a Lambda Chi Alpha and it was the best decision I had ever made. No matter how bad the days were or the practices were, when I went to the frat house, the guys always cheered me up. It was a good reminder that basketball

I didn't get to shoot the ball nearly as much as I would have liked during my time at Indiana because they wanted me to play center all the time.

was just basketball and that there were other parts to life. I had to remind myself every day that Coach can't kill me, that it's just a game. It was a very hard season to deal with, and I was glad I had the fraternity to escape to when I needed to. I didn't live at the house, but I spent a lot of time there and I really needed it.

Part of being an Indiana player is knowing that you're going to wind up in Coach's doghouse now and then. It sure happened to me a lot and, frankly, it happens to everybody. How you survive at Indiana is how you deal with the bad times and being in the doghouse.

Ricky thought he was too good to be in Coach's doghouse or to spend any time there and so when it happened to him – like it did to all of us – he created a huge controversy and dissention among the players. Basketball wise, it was just miserable.

It didn't start that way. When practice started for the 1988 season, Coach was still in a pretty great mood. Winning does that. He was in a great mood and the atmosphere was great. And then we got off to a good start. We were ranked either No. 5 or No. 6 in the first month of the season and our only loss early was against Kentucky in overtime in Indianapolis, which is never good. We played like shit a few weeks later and got beat pretty bad by Louisville, but we finished the nonconference part of the schedule 8-2, which wasn't horrible.

But then the Big Ten season started and we lost four out of our five games and we looked like shit doing it. Even our only win during that stretch was a two-point win over a bad Wisconsin team, where we only scored 55 points. We were horrible and Coach was starting to lose it.

I started most of the time unless I would get into Coach's doghouse, which would happen. We just weren't very good. We weren't playing well so it went from us having a lot of fun the year before to almost back to where we were in '86 and you had those same feelings.

Ricky couldn't handle being in Coach's doghouse. It's what everybody goes through. You just try to keep your mind focused and hopefully get out and move on. But when Ricky got in the trouble, he thought he was too good to be a doghouse and all he ever did was complain to everyone about unfair it was. It wasn't like Ricky did something horrible off the court or was being defiant or anything, but he just wasn't playing well and he wasn't working hard and that was driving Coach nuts. There's nothing Coach hates more than his best players not being the hardest workers, and that was definitely the case with Ricky. He always seemed like he was coasting and that drove Coach crazy.

*** *** ***

And, of course, when Coach gets mad at one person, he's mad at everybody. Each practice continued to get uglier and uglier. Most people think that coaches try to treat every player the same, but that's just not true. And it's definitely not true with Coach Knight. In fact, it's probably just the opposite. With each and every individual, he's going to push you as far as he thinks you can handle. And the better players? He pushed even harder to get the best out of them. But if you didn't work hard, or if you smarted off all the time like Ricky did, well, Coach just didn't go for that. My junior year, it was beyond belief after a while. Every practice turned into a shouting match and he just ripped and ripped and ripped on everyone. There wasn't anyone who avoided it and I'm pretty sure there wasn't a single player that Coach was happy with that year.

I found myself going home and breaking down several

times, and I would tell myself over and over that this is just a game. And he can't kill me. And for me to have that mindset, I had already been defeated. When you get down yourself, it's tough. I hate words like confidence and potential because when you get down to it, either you can play or you can't. But it does make it harder when you're beaten down. So when you get down on yourself, I think Coach sees that and he feeds off it. He can sense it, and he doesn't put up with it with older players. Freshmen, he'll give them a break when they're down because they're still learning the way, but he doesn't like seeing older players feeling that way.

That's why he was so unhappy with Dean and Keith that year, because even though they were playing OK, they weren't making everyone else better. We were sort of leaderless. At one practice, Coach was really upset with Keith and Dean and told them they played like dogs so he wanted them to run like a dog.

As practice ended, Coach had Keith and Dean running sprints and since they were playing like dogs according to Coach, he wanted them to bark like a dog when they ran. So here is Dean and Keith, running sprints and barking like a dog. At one point, Coach had screamed at them, telling them to bark like a god-damned big dog and not a poodle. An hour later, Dean and Keith were still running and barking louder and louder like a big dog.

We finished 11-7 in the Big Ten that year, good for fifth place. We wound up being a No. 4 seed in the NCAA Tournament, which was a bit of a surprise, but we played like crap and lost in the first round to No. 13 seed Richmond. I played OK, scoring 11 points on 4 of 5 shooting and Keith had a good game. Dean really struggled, and on the ride home, we all felt the same way.

We were glad the season was over.

Coach went nuts after that loss too, and I think he might have been just as glad to be rid of us, too. You never felt any love that year and you felt like you were in a battle every day. I was thinking about in 2016 after Indiana lost to North Carolina in the NCAA Tournament. There was a picture of Tom Crean comforting one of his players, Thomas Bryant, in the locker room after the loss. Coach Knight would have thrown us through the wall if he could have. We didn't get hugs. Ever.

There was never any unity on that team, and it was so different from the year before, when everybody did everything together. It just wasn't that way. And then when the year ended, Coach met with the team and I remember everybody wanted Ricky gone. Coach asked everyone and we were all on the same page, even the other black guys. We all wanted Ricky out. Everyone was tired of Ricky throwing gasoline on every fire. He left and went to Kansas and even though Ricky could play, we were a better team without him and that showed the next year.

12

Chapter

A DIFFICULT
SENIOR YEAR AT INDIANA

I could probably write an entire book on my senior year at Indiana, there was that much going on. A lot of it was good, but a lot of it was horrible, too.

I played well most of the season, but then I had to deal with getting benched and landing in Coach Knight's doghouse for several weeks. I was the brunt of his anger several times that season, and it got very physical every time. Over the span of one season, all this went on:

* Early in the year, Coach was so mad that he dug his hands into my side while he was standing over me and yelling. He bruised me pretty bad. That happened in New York at the NIT and it was embarrassing as hell. You could see the bruises. He would also stand over you and dig his hands into your groin and squeeze like hell. I had bruises on my thighs, too.

* He broke a clipboard over my head in the Louisville game and shoved me back on the court another time, which photographers caught and the picture wound up in Sports Illustrated.

* He went nose to nose with me and had me pinned up against a wall in a hallway at Assembly Hall. That was all witnessed by a manager, John Martin.

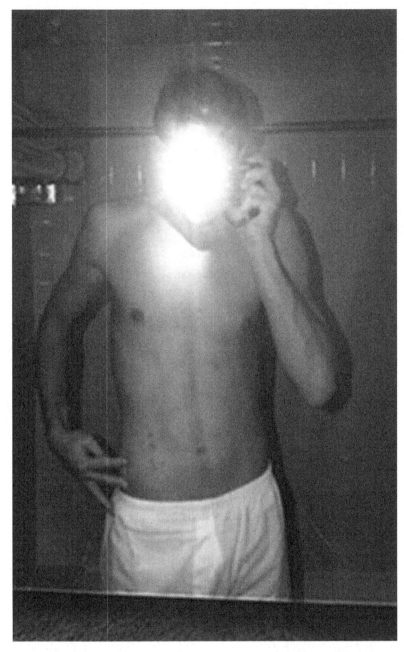

Coach Knight grabbed me so hard that he put bruises on my side during my senior year. I thought it was important to take pictures. You can see where his fingers dug in to me. There's a closer picture to the the right.

* He punched me in the back of the head with a closed fist during a walkthrough for our NCAA regional game. My ears were ringing for several days from that punch. I was ready to quit right there on the spot.

Yeah, it was pretty bad. But it's Indiana and it's Coach Knight, so it was pretty good, too. Picked in the preseason to be a middle-of-the-pack team in the Big Ten, we would up winning the league and he was named national Coach of the Year. We had no size that year. I was our biggest guy and played center all season, but that really wasn't where my strength was. But I was all we had, so that's how it went. During that time, Coach's recruiting had really started to slip, and we just didn't have any other big guys at all. So every minute I played was at center, and sometimes it was fine, but there were times where it wasn't.

Yep, at Indiana you take the good with the bad.

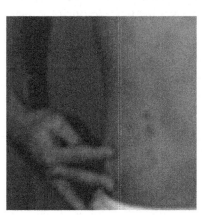

The craziness started right away. Our first game, against Illinois State, I scored 21 and was our leading scorer, which set my expectations pretty high. In the preseason NIT, which was a huge deal loaded with really good teams, I played pretty well and made the all-tournament team. But in one stretch where we weren't playing very well, Coach grabbed me so hard in the game that I had taken a picture of my sides after the game in the hotel. You could see the black bruises of every finger mark that he left from grabbing me so hard in the game against Syracuse in Madison Square Garden. I have pictures of the hand marks and bruises that

I took in the hotel. He went crazy. He said "You're a f------ senior and a captain and it's your responsibility to get these guys playing." As he's yelling this at me, he's squeezing the heck out of my side.

We weren't very good at the beginning of the year, which meant Coach was in a bad mood the whole time. We lost to Syracuse and North Carolina in the NIT in New York, and we gave up more than 100 points in each loss. I played really well in the North Carolina game, though. I had 27 points and the game was on national TV, so I had a lot of friends talking to me about it afterward. We lost to Louisville a few weeks later in Indianapolis, and they scored 100 on us too. For a defensive guy like Coach Knight, that just literally drove him nuts.

That was pretty bad, but that wasn't all of it. There was much, much more.

In the Louisville game in Indy, I made a complete fool out of myself and wound up getting my picture on the cover of Sports Illustrated because of it. The picture is of Coach pushing me back out on the court, but in this case, I deserved it.

It was just one of those moments where you're so consumed with what's going on in the game and worrying so much about not making a mistake. Coach already had been really mad at me and he took a clipboard and busted it over my head and started mocking me because of my tics. He started making fun of me. I remember that game well because I was so out of it after what happened at the timeout with the clipboard.

So there's another timeout and Coach is yelling at me and I thought for sure he had taken me out of the game. I'm just walking to the bench with my head down. Well, of course, he hadn't taken me out of the game; he was just giving me an earful. So he shoves me back out onto the court to stay in the game and everyone gets a great picture of it. And there it winds up, on the cover of Sports Illustrated. I felt horrible about all of that.

I had played really well in the preseason and then when the Big Ten started, I just don't know what happened to me. I got so worried about making mistakes and I wasn't really focusing on the game and what was going on. My numbers went down and everything was starting to spin out of control.

It was really bad when I missed a dunk in a game against Wisconsin and then the next day in practice I missed another dunk and he went nuts and threw me out of practice. I left, but then Coach starts following me down the hall, still yelling and screaming. I'm kicked out and walking to the locker room and Coach gets a rack of balls and one by one he starts firing them at me. He hit me several times and then he chased me down the hallway. I thought Coach and I were going to come to blows as he chased me down. Our trainer, Tim Garl, was there and Coach went right through him, throwing him to the side to get to me. We squared off in the tunnel by the locker room and his face was an inch from mine as he went after me. He was really yelling and screaming, and spitting in my face the whole time. One of the managers, John Martin, was down there and he saw the whole thing.

That was just the start of it. After that, he proceeded to my locker and took out all my belongings, ripped my name plate off my locker and threw everything out into the hall. He said I was done. I think I surprised him by standing up to him because when he started yelling at me, I stood there nose to nose with him. I thought for sure he was going to punch me, he was that angry.

I went home and a few hours later he sent the managers after me. They pounded on my doors till midnight and I finally answered. I went back to Assembly Hall about one o'clock in the morning, only to find his new wife Karen there to talk with me.

They had gotten married the previous summer. We had a candid conversation, and I told her that her husband was flat-out crazy. I don't recall her disagreeing with me.

So the next day after practice, Coach tried relating some stories to me about how I needed to be tougher and that I couldn't disappear in games and all that, never once apologizing for what he did. He just turned it all on me, that because I was playing bad, that's why he got so mad. It was never him; always us.

Near the end of the season, I got punched with a closed fist in the back of the head at a walkthrough as we were preparing to play Seton Hall in the regionals of the NCAA tournament. I walked off the court and quit after that. I remember walking off the floor saying I've had it, that I'm done. Joby Wright, our assistant coach, was screaming at me, "Todd where are you going? You can't leave, you can't quit now. I went into the locker room, got my stuff and went home.

I just kept telling myself that this is just a game and he can't hurt me. Again came the managers pounding at my door, saying coach wants to see you. I said tell him to screw it, that I didn't deserve to get punched. I held out till midnight again, but the managers were relentless and they took me back to Assembly Hall and Coach sort of on his terms apologized for hitting me. That's the closest I've ever seen him come to saying he was sorry for anything.

I sort of hit the wall late in the Big Ten season and wound up getting benched for four games after that incident in practice with Coach. Just to screw with me, he would put me in the game in the last minute if it wasn't close, just to screw with my stats. After the games, he would relay some sort of story to us that was subliminally aimed at me, but I was so mad that I didn't care about his dumb-ass stories.

He totally lost it after we lost at home to Illinois. Coach ripped the sink off the wall and water went everywhere. He tipped over the slush machine and broke all the flavored bottles and stuff went everywhere. It was a mess and Coach had stuff all over him. He had to go in the shower and change. The game ended at 2 p.m. and we didn't get home until 3 a.m.

It was a nightmare, and it really made a lot of us mad because we all had family in town for the game and we never got to see them. We'd watch video, then practice, then come in and watch more video and then more practice. Three in the morning before we finally get out of there. It was so stupid. I had some family there and I never even saw them that day. I saw them for maybe ten minutes the next day and that was it.

Right after that, I was put back into starting lineup and had 32 points, 12 rebounds and tied the record for consecutive free throws made with 18 in a big win against Iowa. It was another one of the crazy mental mind games that he plays with you. I sat on my butt on the bench for four game and then all of a sudden, I'm back in the starting lineup and he's telling me he's going to give me another chance.

Well, it worked. We won seven in a row and wound up winning the Big Ten. We found a good rhythm and then we started winning. I don't know how to explain it. We were playing great and it continued to snowball for us. We became a very cohesive unit and we really played well together. We started winning every game and we expected to win every time we walked into the gym.

I was playing so well that my emotions even got me in trouble with Coach during that stretch. We were up at Minnesota for a game, and that's a really hard place to win. We had a chance to clinch the Big Ten but the day before I had hurt my ankle really bad. It was all black and blue and I had a stress fracture and got

treatment all night long. I wasn't about to miss that game. Anyway, we're playing great and we're winning big and I get open and go in for a big dunk. I slam it down hard and get fouled, and I'm all wound up. Afterward, I pump my fist real big – kind of like an animated Tiger Woods fist pump – and sort of let my emotions get the best of me, just celebrating a little too much, you know. The crowd's getting all over me, because they were wound up too, being a big game and all on national TV. Coach takes me out and just lights into me on the bench, yelling and screaming at me for showing off like "a f----- NFL running back who just found the end zone." I never went back in the game and then in the locker room afterward, he wanted me to apologize to my teammates for trying to show them up. I couldn't help it. What can I say? I got caught up in the moment.

My most embarrassing moment on the floor that season came against Iowa, though. Iowa loved to press a lot and they aggressively covered the inbounds passer, which was me a lot of the time. It used to drive Coach nuts that they would reach over the baseline all the time – and not just their arms; their whole body would be over the line – and the referees would never call it. He'd yell and scream but the refs ignored him.

So Coach instructed me to throw the ball off the face of the Iowa player if he crossed the end line. Coach did the same thing a year earlier. He made Daryl Thomas throw a ball off the face of Iowa's Brad Lohaus, and that became a big thing, too.

So Kent Hill was guarding me, and he kept coming over the line, so I did what Coach said and fired the ball right into his face. I hit him hard and his nose was all bloody. He came up swinging and got ejected from the game. Nothing happened to me; in fact, I went down to shoot the technical foul shots.

But I tell you what, I felt horrible about it, even if Coach

95

IN THEIR OWN WORDS

Mark Robinson, Indiana (1988-90)

I enjoyed my time with Todd at Indiana and he was definitely a unique teammate. He wasn't all caught up in being an Indiana player and was never cocky.

Todd had a real challenge in the locker room that I had never encountered before. He had these twitches that were uncontrollable, or so we thought they were. One time Coach Knight was mad at him and he's yelling at Todd and he's just screaming at him "If you don't stoop that f------ twitching, I'm going to throw your ass out of here. Todd stopped, and we didn't know how he did that. We all knew that was Todd's disorder, but from Coach's perspective, he never looked at it that way. Coach yelled at everybody though, picked on everybody, treated everybody the same. Todd was just in the way some days.

I played overseas for a lot of years too, so I know all about Todd's experiences over there in Europe and then South America. It's a different lifestyle over there and it's not for everybody.

We both are in fields now where we are reaching out to help others, and it's good to get reconnected with Todd and see that he's doing well. Society is on the verge of embracing what I'm doing and I'm sure people are going to enjoy listening to Todd tell his stories.

Dr. Mark Robinson played two seasons at Indiana and is now a sports counselor who lives in Walnut Creek, California.

ordered me to do it. I felt so bad that I sent an apology letter to Iowa coach Tom Davis and Kent. We had to play at Iowa at the end of the season, and we had already clinched the Big Ten so Coach sat all the starters. It was probably a good thing for me, because there probably would have been some retribution.

Senior nights at Indiana are something special, and mine was too, of course. We beat Wisconsin that night and had already won the Big Ten with one game to go at Iowa. We all talked a lot about our speeches that night and mine went off pretty well. I wasn't too nervous. Coach stole the show, of course, when he came up with a line that's been watched on YouTube and other places probably five millions times. His line? "When my time on earth is gone, and my activities here are past, I want they bury me upside down, and my critics can kiss my ass." No doubt, that's the perfect Coach Knight summation.

Telling everybody to kiss his ass seemed about right for him. That was the thing about Coach, he felt like he didn't have to answer to anybody and, quite frankly, he didn't. The perfect example of that was the year before, when we were playing the Russian national team in an exhibition game. Coach Knight was having a rough night with the referees, and we were playing horrible and getting our butts kicked. When he finally got his third technical foul and was ejected from the game, he just went nuts. He pulled us off the floor and wouldn't let us go back out there. It was embarrassing as hell.

Turns out, he wouldn't budge either when the athletic director came in. He wouldn't let us play and we had to forfeit the game. Coach had total and complete control, so much so that he basically cancelled a game right in the middle of it. It didn't help that we were losing 66-43 with 15 minutes remaining. He was probably more upset with us for playing bad than he was with the refs. There were a lot of crazy things Coach did during my time at Indiana but that ranked right up there for being stubborn and crazy. I mean, that's nuts, right? Just taking your team off the court in the middle of the game? Totally nuts.

We won our first two games in the NCAA Tournament, which was nice, but then we lost to Seton Hall in the regional finals. And that was that. It was just one of those nights where we didn't play very well and it was too bad, because we had really been on a roll.

Seton Hall wound up making it all the way to the national championship game that year, where they lost to Michigan. That really kind of hurt us, because that was more proof to us that maybe we could have won it all that year. I mean, Michigan won it all and we beat them twice during the season. It was only by one point each time, but still, wins are wins. There's no doubt we felt we were better than Michigan that year, but they got the rings. That was a year where we missed out on hanging a banner. We were that good.

When it was all said and done, my four years at Indiana were memorable and unforgettable. For all the run-ins I had with Coach Knight, I'm still glad I chose to play for him, even though I had my doubts along the way – several times. He made me a better player and I learned a lot about growing up by being there.

Still, I was glad it was over. That year, all of us seniors, we kept a running countdown in our notebooks about how many days we had left putting up with Coach. In a few weeks, I would leave Bloomington to start my new life, and I had a big smile on my face as I drove away from Bloomington.

I wouldn't come back for more than 25 years.

13

Chapter

MY PARTY
LIFE AT INDIANA

There is no doubt that Bloomington is one of the best
college towns in America. People get great educations at Indiana,
but they also have a lot of fun. It was certainly no different for us
back in the late 1980s. There was always a party to get to, always a
beer to be had, always something stronger if you wanted it.

It was a good thing to be an Indiana basketball player, but
there were some bad parts to it, too. Everyone wanted to party with
us, and it was a big deal if some of us came to a party. But there
was always one reason why we kept it pretty much under control.

That one reason? The wrath of Coach Knight.

That was reason enough to keep a low profile if we wanted
to have a drink or two. During the season, quite frankly, you were
too exhausted to be out all night acting crazy. But a little fun
here and there was never a bad thing. A lot of us lived together in
apartments at Jackson Heights. We knew a lot of our neighbors, so
whenever they were having parties, they would always make sure
to let us know. They wanted us to be there, and for us it was easy
to be there, too.

We'd always see a lot of girls at these parties, obviously.
And when we didn't come to them, they'd come to us. The girls
knew where we lived, and they'd be coming by our doors all the

time. Having a girl come back to my apartment after a party there at Jackson Heights was nothing. It happened all the time. And even if we weren't out somewhere, girls would always come by our apartments. They would leave little gifts or mementos, and they left names and phone numbers all the time. And when I mean all the time, I mean ALL … THE … TIME. Access to really cute girls might have been the best perk of being an Indiana basketball player, at least during my days there.

One of the best things I ever did at Indiana was join a fraternity. There were a lot of days it was a real life-saver for me. In '88 or so, I became good friends with Adam Grose and he was the president of the Lambda Chi Alpha fraternity. I got to know several of the guys in Lambda Chi and they were fun to hang out with.

I didn't live in the house, but I went over there quite bit. No matter how bad days were at practice, I could go over there

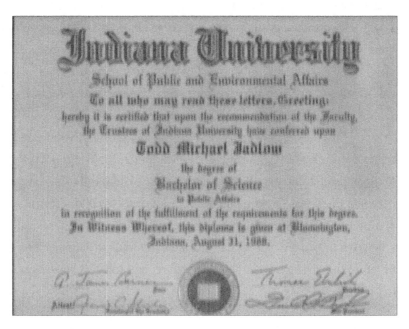

I was proud to play basketball at Indiana, but I'm also proud of being a good student for four years and earning this diploma.

afterward and just chill out. We had fun and nobody bothered me. People would cheer you up and make sure you could forget about all the crap in your day. It was my great escape place.

I didn't have to go through all the usual rush stuff. I was an IU player and they really wanted me in the house, so I was fortunate. I didn't do the whole rush week stuff, or the pledge things that everyone else has to go through. They had a secret private house meeting and they took a vote and it was unanimous that they wanted me. If one person would have said no, then I would have been out. Thankfully no one did, so I became a "Lamb Chop."

There were a lot of really good guys in that house. I would go over there quite a bit and have dinner with everyone. I did a lot of things for people there, too. Because my family hardly ever came to games, I would give my tickets to guys at the fraternity. At that time in my life, it was great be around that atmosphere. It was all so different from basketball, where everything was so strict and regimented. At the fraternity, we just crashed and had fun. I really needed that at that point in my life.

We had a lot of fun parties there. There were always a lot of girls around at their parties and I met a lot of really fun girls there. That was always nice. There were also a lot of drugs at those parties, but I never did any. That's one thing I never did during my four years in college. I never did drugs of any kind. I wasn't about to embarrass myself or the IU program, so I always stayed away from drugs.

The only drugs I ever took in college that were illegal were steroids. A lot of the football guys used them back then and they hooked me up. I took them during the summer the year after I redshirted and it made a big difference with my body. I took two cycles over a two-month period and I probably gained 20 pounds or so. Iit was all muscle. You could see it in my chest and my arms and I really noticed the difference in pictures from practice and everything over time. It made a big difference in my size. I really didn't know anything about steroids at all, and I had no idea about all the side effects they could have. If I had known all that at the time, I probably wouldn't have taken them.

So I stuck to drinking if I was going to do anything. I always kept it in control back then though, because I was so scared of Coach Knight. I saw a lot of alcohol abuse around me though. There were a lot of guys in the fraternity who were way over the top with their alcohol abuse. Yeah, I know it's college, but there were a lot of really hard drinkers in that place.

We never really partied hard as a team, although a few of us would have drinks together now and then. One time that really stood out was went we got invited to John Mellencamp's house for a party back in 1987 and that was a blast. He was a huge rock star at the time and he's from Southern Indiana and loves everything about IU. He got in touch with Steve and a bunch of us went out to his house and drank beer out of coolers and ate and played some hoops on an outdoor court he had there at the house, with him and his band mates. It was very cool.

He always liked having us around and he would come to a bunch of games too. Some of the guys actually would go with him on the bus tour when he was on tour doing concerts. His "Scarecrow" album had just come out the first time I met him, and a lot of us bought albums and had him autograph them so we could give them away for Christmas gifts. Man, those were big hits.

One thing that a lot of people never realized with Coach Knight was that as strict as he was, there were very few written rules. What you could do – or couldn't do – was really just handed down from one group to the next. We didn't have set curfews or had to be locked into our apartments or things like that.

One of the unwritten rules was that we were supposed to stay out of the bars in Bloomington, especially during the season. That was an absolute no-no. We were able to go down to Kirkwood Avenue or College Avenue and hang around, and we could go places where we could get a bite to eat and all, but you just couldn't get caught drinking in there, even though the owners loved having us there. The '87 season was a good example of that. We had a lot of fun off the court that year, too. I mean, everybody was in a good mood. We were having a great season and Coach was in a good mood and it was just fun. Hanging out in Bloomington was fun for a basketball player, but if we were going to have a drink or two, we always did it far out of view of the general public. We pretty much kept that to the apartments and the frat houses.

One time Dean Garrett and Keith Smart went down inside a bar during my junior year and it was obvious the reach Coach Knight had around town. They were only in that bar a few minutes and right away the owners were on the phone with the basketball office, calling and saying "Do you know your players are in here?" That was something we just couldn't do. That's why we went to a lot of fraternity parties. We could have our fun without going nuts and nobody really said anything. It was nice too, because there were always a lot of girls around at those parties.

That was always a good thing.

Staying out of trouble was always important. Not everyone cared all the time though. During my senior year, Jay Edwards failed a drug test before the season started and that really pissed Coach Knight off. Jay was a great, great player, but he was a pain in the ass and he drove Coach nuts. When he failed that drug test, it scared all of us. I never did any drugs back then, and that was a good reason why.

That would come later. But not much later.

103

14

Chapter

COACH KNIGHT'S
PARADE OF CELEBRITIES

Back in those days in the 1980s, there might not have been a bigger celebrity in college basketball than Coach Knight. He was as big as they come, even outside of basketball. But Coach Knight also had a lot of celebrity friends and they were around Bloomington all the time. It was pretty cool that we got to meet them all.

Some people were sort of local, and we would see them quite a bit. Fuzzy Zoeller, the golfer who won The Masters in 1979, was from southern Indiana and he never left. He was a huge supporter of all things Indiana, and he was a big fan of Coach and our team. He would come up to games a lot, but he'd stop by practice too every once in a while. He was a nice guy and he always had a funny story or two to tell. I didn't really know much about him because I didn't really follow golf, but it was good to get to know him.

There was another golfer who came by once and it was kind of embarrassing for me. Curtis Strange came to practice one time. He had just won two U.S. Opens in a row – nobody has done that since – but when he was introduced to us, I had absolutely no idea who the guy was. A U.S. Open champ, and I didn't even know

105

IU Archives P0059085dit

My coach, Bob Knight, really knew how to work a room, even a big one like Assembly Hall. It's an honor to be called a Bob Knight player.

106

it. He took me out to dinner, just him and I, during my slump my senior year and he told a bunch of stories and I'm thinking, man, I don't even know who this guy is. But Coach made a point of showing him around and you could tell Coach liked having him there. He was a nice guy and he really seemed to enjoy being around us, too.

Coach is a huge baseball fan and there were a lot of baseball legends around all the time. Johnny Bench, the great catcher of the Cincinnati Reds, didn't live far away and he came up to Bloomington quite a bit. We got to meet him all the time. Tony LaRussa, the great manager, would always come for a visit before he left for spring training. He and Coach always had a lot of respect for each other. They would all come to speak to us, and it was pretty cool. D. Wayne Lucas, the famous horse trainer, was a big fan of Coach's too, and he'd come by a lot and offer us tickets to the Kentucky Derby as his guest. I think it meant a lot to Coach too, to have them come talk to us.

A lot of basketball people came by all the time. Former Indiana players were there constantly and whenever they were there they used to all tell us how easy we had it compared to Coach Knight back in their day. I get the feeling that every Indiana player says that, that their time was always the worst with Coach.

Former coaching legends would always stop in for a day or two. Coach, for as tough as he was, always had a soft spot for those older coaches who taught him a lot on the way up. He'd pick their brains a lot, but he was also a good friend to those guys. Whenever they were in town, Coach always made a big deal out of it, and showed them a lot of respect. He made sure we did the same thing.

It was the same with NFL coaches. Dick Vermeil, who's coached in some Super Bowls, came by a lot. Another celebrity who was as big a name as Coach Knight back then was Bill Parcells. He was the coach of the New York Giants in the NFL and a Super Bowl champion. He and Coach Knight were at Army at the same time and they became good friends. That was certainly understandable, because they were very similar as coaches, really tough on their players, really smart about how to win games, really organized and attentive to make sure nothing ever fell through the cracks. They were good friends and after football season ended, we'd see Coach Parcells quite a bit and he and Coach were always talking and laughing and telling stories. He'd have Coach Parcells talk to us every time he was there. He would always bring Giants gear for us, which was nice.

Coach and I used to go back and forth quite a bit on Coach Parcells, and it was one of the few times I could bust Coach's chops a little bit. I was a big 49ers fan back then and the first year I got there, I remember Coach going on and on about how Parcells and his Giants killed the 49ers in the playoffs. They did too, it was like 49-3. But going forward the 49ers were the team and they won a couple of Super Bowls, and I would remind Coach about that a time or two. Especially my last two years there, the 49ers were rolling, and those were the years Coach was really on me all the time. So I'd throw it back at him, how the Giants sucked and all and how great the 49ers were. Parcells was his friend and I don't think Coach liked me cracking on him like that, but at the time I didn't really care. I really hated him them, those stretches where he was all over me.

What was nice about having celebrities around at practice is that Coach was usually in a pretty good mood when they were around, which meant a lot of the crap that usually went on wouldn't happen, or at least wouldn't happen as much. There'd be lots of times where we'd just have a nice, snappy one-hour practice and that would be that and Coach would be on his way. So, yeah, having those guys come by was something we all always looked forward to.

Coach was a huge hunter and fisherman and a lot of his buddies were guys he did all that outdoor stuff with. So with Coach and his buddies, you never knew when a good hunting or fishing story would come up. Coach was even pretty good at relating one thing or another to basketball. We'd all really shake our heads most of the time, but a lot of time he was spot on, too.

One time we came to practice and there was a note on the white-board that said "No tape." That was always nice, because it usually meant we were just going to walk through some things and not go live. That was a nice thing for us, because so many times all practice meant was two or three hours of pure hell. Having an easy day now and then was a good thing.

So we go no tape and dress out and when we head out to the court, Coach is out there all dressed up from head to toe in his old fishing gear. He's got his waders on, his hat, fishing pole, everything. It was quite a vision. He's got his fly rod and he's just casting away, like 50 or 60 feet or so. So while he's doing that, he tells us to sit down and then he starts in on us. When you fish, he says, you have to fish with purpose. And when you f----- cut across the lane, you have to do it with purpose. You just don't start stepping your toe in the water and running around and scaring all the fish. You do it with purpose. He goes on and on, one thing after another relating fishing to basketball and doing things right.

This went on for two hours. After it was done, Coach went on his way and we went back to the locker room after not even practicing a bit. We basically watched him fly-fish and tell stories for two hours, but I guess that's what fishermen do. They tell stories.

You never knew with Coach. It was always interesting.

15

Chapter

PICKING AN AGENT FOR ME
AND FINDING A NEW TEAM

After the season ended, Coach Knight called me into his office. I was shocked that the first thing he did was apologize for playing me out of position for my last two years. You know, in my mind, I think Coach felt bad about the way he had used me and that it was probably going to cost me some money at the next level. Those last two years – and that last year especially – he wanted me to play center and in our offense, that meant that you stayed down low and didn't get involved in the offense on the perimeter at all. I had never done that. I had never been a center, and in high school and junior college I was always a shooter. If you go back and look at my stats for my freshman year at Barton, you'll see I made a lot of three-pointers. But during my time at Indiana, I didn't take any. And then I go off to Europe and that's all I do is shoot.

When he brought up the subject of agents, he had a whole stack of letters from agents and he basically recommended to me who I should go with. There were all those letters there from dozens of agents, but Coach basically said. "This is who I want you to go with. I know this guy is a good guy and he will take good care of you." I didn't even really look at any of the letters in the stack. I just took Coach's suggestion and left it at that.

Coach wanted me to use Larry Fleischer at International

111

Management Group as my agent. He was one of the biggest agents around at the time and so was IMG. They represented a lot of basketball players, but they were huge beyond basketball too, and everyone in sports knew who Larry Fleisher was. They represented the best tennis players and golfers too, and had lots of great contacts all over the world. They were big time. Based on what I had done in college, I probably wasn't the type of client that they would normally take, but Mr. Fleisher really liked Coach Knight and if Coach asked him to take me, I'm sure Larry wasn't going to say no. He represented a lot of All-Stars and he was also president of the NBA Players Association.

Larry's office was in New York City, right down there in Manhattan right by Central Park. I flew to New York to meet with him, and it was first class all the way. We went to lunch at a nice restaurant in Manhattan. We talked a lot about Coach Knight and my time at Indiana and I really liked him. He was really impressive. He really made me feel like he would take good care of me and look out after me. He even made of point of telling me that he would take care of me personally, because I was a Coach Knight player and that meant a lot to him. That made me feel pretty comfortable with him.

I could tell he had already been doing his homework on me and had been asking around the league about me. He had already mentioned the New Jersey Nets to me and he knew that they had been there at the World University Games when I was trying out for a team that Mike Kryzyzewski from Duke was coaching. Willis Reed, who was running things for the Nets at the time, had been there watching all the practices and I think he liked my game.

I really liked Larry and I signed with him the next day, and I was really happy about it.

***   ***   ***

I spent the early part of the summer training and getting ready for the draft up near Indianapolis. That summer was also my introduction to cocaine. I tried it for the first time that summer, and the person who introduced it to me was a teammate that still had another year left at IU.

He called me over to his house and he said he had something for me. It was cocaine. So I tried it, and I liked it. There was something about doing this taboo thing that kind of drew you in, being illegal and all. I had never seen it before in my life and I had never tried to buy it or anything.

I knew it was wrong from the get-go and that's why later in the year when I started to do it more often, I always hid it and didn't say anything to anybody. But I really liked it. I liked the feeling you got from it. I knew it was wrong the whole time I was doing it, but it was my goal to keep it as private as possible as to who knew I was taking it. I only did it with other players. I was always extremely cautious because of the legal ramifications. And paranoid too.

***   ***   ***

After I met with Larry Fleisher in New York, I flew back home and I think it was either the next day or the day after, and I was in my apartment at night with a girlfriend of mine. We were just hanging out watching TV with a few people.

And so as we're watching CNN, across the ticker on the bottom of the screen comes this note that Larry Fleisher, the head of the NBA Players Association, had died of a massive heart attack in New York while playing racquetball at his health club in New York. I'm looking at everyone and thinking, ''You've got to be kidding me.'' I had just signed with him, had just seen him in New York. I really felt bad for him, and I had really been looking forward to working with him because I knew he was going to take good care of me.

From then on, everything changed for me with IMG. I don't know, I just think I got lost in the mix. Eric Fleisher, Larry's son, took over with me, but I got the impression right from the beginning that he really didn't care about me all that much. It was like night and day between Eric and his Dad, because Larry had this great relationship Coach Knight already and it seemed like Eric didn't know anything about me.

Nothing about Eric impressed me at all. He had some big-time players like Orlando Woodridge and I was just a kid to him. He told me there were a few teams interested and when draft night came around, there was a chance I would get drafted in the second round. That was the first year that the draft was only two rounds. The Nets seemed to be the team most interested, and he told me that they were trying to decide if they were going to take me or Stanley Brundy, who played at DePaul in Chicago. I waited and waited on draft night, and when the Nets' pick came around the second round, they decided to take Brundy. I was really disappointed. The rest of the draft came and went, and no one picked me.

Later that night after the draft ended, the Nets called and wanted to let me know that they were still really interested in me. They said they really wanted me to come to camp with them. They laid it on pretty heavy, telling me that they've been watching me for two years and they think I could help them and all that. Not enough to draft me, of course, but to sign me afterward. It would have been nice to have been able to say I was drafted, but that just didn't happen.

Eric and I talked it over and I wound up signing with the Nets to go to camp. There were no guarantees that I would make the team, of course, but that's the way they talked, that they liked my game enough to be able to stick around. So I fly to New Jersey and when I got there, I couldn't believe it. There were like 60 people there for the camp to try out. It wasn't what they had told me at all. The deal was they were going to try out all of us and then take six people to Los Angeles for their summer league, along with some of their current players.

Thankfully I played really well and I was one of the six picked to go to LA. It was a pretty cool situation. It was fun being in Los Angeles and we worked really hard. We practiced a lot and played games. I was scoring in double figures and rebounding well and – most importantly – I was really shooting the ball well.

That summer with the Nets, one of the coaches – Butch Beard – came over to me and said, "Man, we did not know you could shoot like that. Why didn't you shoot at Indiana like that? I told them because the role Coach put me into did not allow for that. And if you played outside your role at Indiana, you wouldn't play, so I did what I was told to by the coaches.

Looking back, I truly believe had I gone to another school that would have allowed me to play the way Coach had initially intended for me to play, I would have been a high draft pick. So many variables go into it, but you play the way Coach wants you to play, or you don't play at all. I was never a center or a power forward ever in my life and was not recruited to be such. Coach Knight had always compared my scoring skills to that of Scott May when he talked about me in the press after he recruited me. Scott May was a great scoring forward on those great Indiana teams in the 1970s. I really felt shorted in my college basketball experience

115

that I didn't get to play the way I can. Don't get me wrong, playing for Coach Knight was an honor and something I treasure to this
day, but I just wish I could have played as I was recruited to play at
Indiana.

After about three weeks there with the Nets, I had a guy
from France come watch me play. His name was Didier Rose and
had been watching me for a while and he said, "We want you to
come to France today we'll pay you $100,000 a year." That was a
lot of money for me. I never had any money and it sounded interesting to me.

I called Eric and told him I was thinking about it and he
was mad and didn't think I should leave. The Nets were telling
me that I was in the running for the last spot on the team. It was
between me and a guy named Anthony Mason. He wound up playing in the league for a long time, but he was a jackass and a thug.

I got to make a lot of great trips during my college basketball career, but
there was nothing better than going to the White House and meeting
President Ronald Reagan after winning the national championship.

We got in fights in practice all the time and people had to separate us a lot. He was a dirty player, always giving guys cheap shots in practice, including me. We tried to get some sort of guarantee from Willis Reed. Back then, a lot of people would get at least a $20,000 guarantee to go to the veteran's camp. We were pushing for that because we didn't want to lose this other job. But they weren't willing to give us that guarantee. They kept telling me they really liked me and they kept telling me my chances were good, and I was having fun too. I made some good friends. Chris Morris kind of took me under his wings and showed me the ropes. It was a good situation, but it wasn't a *guaranteed* situation.

And that wasn't good enough for me.

I had to make a decision, because the season in France started right away, before the NBA season started. I was 22 years old and didn't have a penny to my name. Here was somebody offering me guaranteed money, and here were the Nets, offering me a chance but nothing else. It was an NBA chance, and I understood that, but having money in your pocket was a pretty big deal, too.

So I picked France. And that was that.

I was officially a professional basketball player.

16

Chapter

HEADING OFF TO EUROPE
FOR PRO BALL

I got over to France, to this town called Caen that was right on the English Channel and just a few miles from Normandy, which everyone knows from the World War II invasion. It was a nice place, a city of about 100,000 people or so, but the whole metro area was about 400,000. It was big enough, and nice enough.

I played really well over there right from the beginning. Here's how all those European leagues work. You are allowed to only have two foreign players on your team, but the rest of the roster is filled out with all French players. Our team wasn't very good, even though we were in the first division. The seasons are different over there, too. They are longer than an NBA season on the calendar, but you don't play nearly as often. There were a lot of times where we would play one game a week. I played about 20 games before I hurt my ankle – the French league season was only 32 games – and I was in the top five in scoring, averaging more than 30 points a game. I scored over 50 several times and even had 69 one night.

The level of competition was pretty low. Our Indiana teams would have beaten everyone in that league by 50 points every night. Everybody was really soft and I could shoot it or take the ball to the basket pretty much any time I wanted. Going from Indiana to France was like going from the military to civilian life. In France, the guys all played really soft. They were all just timid and shy and went away from contact, so I could just dominate.

But then I hurt my ankle pretty bad, as bad as I hurt it when I was at Indiana. It was a huge letdown because I was really enjoying it over there. We were in the lower tier of the first division in the standings, so we weren't going anywhere and there were just a couple of weeks left in the season. So they paid me the rest of my contract and I came back to the States.

I stayed pretty clean in France, for the most part. I partied a little bit, but nothing totally out of control. One time, Derrick Rowland, my American teammate there, had someone mail over some cocaine and we did that a few times. Everybody did it on that team, and we'd get together with other Americans on other teams, and we'd all party together.

The whole American networking system in Europe was pretty incredible. Whatever you needed, you could get. It was just kind of the lifestyle. After every game, you'd get together and have fun. It became a way of life.

***   ***   ***

I **came back to** the States and rehabbed my ankle for a bit. And then Eric Fleisher called me to say he had an offer for me with the Pensacola Tornadoes in the CBA. I was feeling a lot better, so I took it. I went down to Florida and I played for Joe Mullaney there, and he was really good. He used to coach the Los Angeles Lakers and it was a pretty nice set-up for minor league basketball, all things considered. Pensacola is right on the Gulf of

Mexico, so that was nice, too.

I played really well and scored over 30 points a game quite a bit. We had a good team and made the playoffs and we played the Albany Patroons, who were coached at the time by George Karl, who wound up coaching the NBA for a lot of years. They were pretty good, too. Mario Elie, who had a good NBA career, was on their team, and so was Vincent Askew. Derrick Rowland, who played with me in France, grew up in Albany and he told me whenever I was there that I should call his best friend, Keith Rhodes. Mike Tyson, the boxer, was from that area and was friends with Keith too, and when we were playing up there, I got to meet Tyson.

We wound up losing the series but I did get some Mike Tyson memorabilia while I was there. It didn't last very long, but it was fun. I played well and it was nice to be in the U.S., where I got noticed a little bit.

***   ***   ***

When I was done with Pensacola, the New Jersey Nets came calling again. They watched me play a lot of that CBA season and they told me I played extremely well and they wanted me to come back to camp that fall. I said OK and I was excited. It was the same as the year before. I got to New Jersey and there were another 60 or so guys trying out for their summer league team. Just like the year before, they kept six or seven guys and I made the cut again.

We flew to Los Angeles again for the summer league, but this time it was completely different. The year before I played a lot when Butch Beard was coaching the summer league team, but this time I hardly got to play at all and I didn't understand one bit. Bill Fitch was the coach now and everything was completely different.

121

Rick Carlisle was coaching the summer league team that second year, and he barely talked to me. When I was part of the group they picked to go out there, they told me how much they were looking forward to watching me play, but I literally only played a few minutes a game. I wasn't getting any run at all.

I was miserable and I told Eric Fleischer that I wanted out of here. He's like, "Relax, they love you. This is crazy. They want to keep you, so just stay put. You're going to get signed to a contract."

I was just trying to put two and two together, though, and none of it made any sense. They were telling Eric how much they wanted me, but at the same time they weren't showing me any-thing. I wasn't playing at all. They kept telling Eric that they knew I'd be a great practice player and that because I was an Indiana guy, I wasn't going to cause any problems. They were talking about keeping me, but once again they weren't guaranteeing any-thing. They just wanted a practice player.

So, just to be safe, on my own I started calling around to some of the people I met in Europe and I am thinking to myself, to hell with Eric, I'm getting my own job. I just didn't feel like I could trust the Nets, not the way they were ignoring me on the court.

So I just walked away.

Like an idiot, from potentially getting a shot in the NBA with the Nets, I just turned and walked away. I had something lined up in Switzerland, so I told Eric I was going to take it and he was really pissed. He didn't really care about me; he only cared about getting paid and he was mad that I did the whole Switzerland thing on my own. That was the end of my relationship with him.

I fired Eric. In hindsight, it was probably another one of my bad decisions. My whole life I have always made rash decisions and in this case, once again, I chased the sure money instead of following my dream. I took the money and ran off to Switzerland.

But honestly, I wanted the money because at the time I was broke. Well, I wasn't broke like the first year, because I had saved some money from my time in France. But still, I didn't have much. And when you grow up with nothing, that really means something. The money wasn't as good as France, maybe $70,000 instead of $100,000, but that meant the world to me financially.

I just didn't want to take the risk with the Nets. My agent was so pissed, because he couldn't believe I was walking away from a chance at the NBA. I just wanted to play and with the Nets I was probably going to be nothing more than a practice player. I just didn't get caught up in being in the NBA. I wanted to play, and I wanted to get paid. It was probably a bad decision, looking back. It was the NBA and I probably should have done whatever it took to see it out, but you never know. Maybe I would have been more than a practice player.

Or maybe not.

17

Chapter

OFF TO SWITZERLAND
FOR YEAR 2 AS A PRO

After I got the job myself in Europe, I headed off to Switzerland. It really is so different in Europe, how things work. In the U.S., you have your one agent and everything you do, you do that through them. In Europe, I met all sort of agents in France just during my first few months there. There were guys like that all over Europe, so you really could fend for yourself. They liked Indiana players over there too, so when I started asking around, a lot of people knew who I was. This new team was in Bellinzona, Switzerland and it was in the first division of the Swiss League. I didn't make six figures, but it was close. It was still a lot of money to me. The basketball still wasn't a very high level, but we had a good team and we won a lot, so that made it more fun. It's just so different over there, though. The seasons are long, but you don't play that many games compared to an NBA season, and it's not nearly the same grind. There's plenty of time to have fun, in other words.

Bellinzona was beautiful. It was up in the mountains near Logano, and it was gorgeous. It was about an hour or so from Milan, and I really enjoyed it. The quality of play wasn't very good there, and I dominated a lot of the games. Every team is allowed two foreign players and the other American on my team was a

I really enjoyed my time playing professional basketball in Switzerland in the early 1990s. I loved Fribourg, which was a beautiful, clean city.

guy named Willie White, who was from Tennessee-Chattanooga, and he was a shooter. I averaged more than 30 points a game and we qualified for all the big European tournaments and got to play against a lot of the best teams in Europe. We played a team from Spain that had Harold Pressley from Villanova and Corney Thompson from Texas. We weren't good enough to beat those good teams, but at home I remember scoring 49 points against Pressley.

I had an interesting time there. The owner of the team there was a big Mafia guy named Ponzio and he had this really young wife named Sandra who was super hot. Ponzio owned brothels, lots of brothels, so I enjoyed myself there too, to say the least. There were lots of visits to the brothels. After every game, he'd take me to one of the brothels and we'd drink champagne and he'd just tell me to pick out a girl or two.

His ex-wife, who was like 50, was hot, too, and Franca and I had a long romantic liaison for several months. We had some crazy fun times together. She owned her own jewelry store and she constantly designed jewelry for me. She even had a Cartier necklace custom-made for me, which was nice. She was totally into me.

I wound up sleeping with his ex-wife for a long time, and he never knew about it. She was 50, but she was still beautiful. She was like my first sugar momma. Here I was, like 24 years old, and she wanted to marry me and buy me anything. We went out for all sorts of great dinners and I drove her Ferrari, and she told me if I would marry her, that she would buy me any car I wanted. She also had a Mercedes SL 500, which became my dream car. I bought one later in life, and still own it to this day.

It was crazy really, because she lived in this beautiful place right above where her ex-husband had his offices. I'd walk down from my apartment right to hers, and we had a lot of fun. We got really close, but to me, I just thought we were having fun. I was still just a kid, just partying and having a lot of great sex and her pampering me like crazy.

But it was a lot more serious to her. I mean, she was crazy in love with me. And when I told her after the season that I was leaving, jeez, I mean she tried to commit suicide. I always wondered what the owner thought, because he had to know I was with her all the time. It's probably amazing that he didn't kill me.

I never used any drugs in Bellinzona, but I definitely drank a lot at parties. But it was nothing big at all.

18

Chapter

ONE WOMAN IN AT FRIBOURG, ANOTHER ONE SENT HOME

After that year in Bellinzona, I never even thought about
going to go back to the States and trying to hook up with an NBA
team. I don't really know why, other than the fact that I was really
enjoying my life over there in Switzerland. An American coach
from Fribourg, Switzerland wanted me to come play for them. It
was for more money, too, which is always good. I mean, it's the
early 1990s, it's about $80,000, and it's all tax free. And Fribourg
is a beautiful city, which is like 15 minutes outside of Bern. So I
took it and I was happy about it, because I liked the idea of staying
in Switzerland. It's a beautiful country.

The other American on the team was a guy named Billy
Martin. He was from Georgetown, and he played on those great
teams in the 1980s with Patrick Ewing and Horace Broadnax and
David Wingate. Billy and I became really close and we had a lot
of fun together. We had a really good team there and wound up
winning the league championship. I played for Joe Welton, who
was from Connecticut and was a really good coach. I averaged 30
points a night and it was a fun stop.

We won the Swiss Cup in Switzerland, along with winning
the league. We also played in the Korac Cup, which was European
tournament for third-level teams across the continent. We didn't

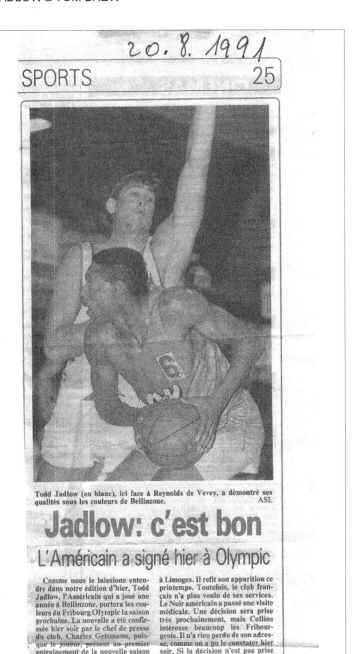

20. 8. 1991

SPORTS 25

Todd Jadlow (en blanc), ici face à Reynolds de Vevey, a démontré ses qualités sous les couleurs de Bellinzone. ASL

Jadlow: c'est bon

L'Américain a signé hier à Olympic

Comme nous le laissions entendre dans notre édition d'hier, Todd Jadlow, l'Américain qui a joué une année à Bellinzone, portera les couleurs du Fribourg Olympic la saison prochaine. La nouvelle a été confirmée hier soir par le chef de presse du club, Charles Geismann, puisque le joueur, présent au premier entraînement de la nouvelle saison hier soir, a signé un contrat d'une à Limoges. Il refit son apparition ce printemps. Toutefois, le club français n'a plus voulu de ses services. Le Noir américain a passé une visite médicale. Une décision sera prise très prochainement, mais Collins intéresse beaucoup les Fribourgeois. Il n'a rien perdu de son adresse, comme on a pu le constater hier soir. Si la décision n'est pas prise cette semaine, Collins fera vraisem-

It's always nice to get your name in the newspaper, even when it's in a foreign language. They wrote about me a lot in Switzerland.

130

win but I played well. I scored 46 one night against Toni Kukoc, who later played with the Chicago Bulls in the NBA for a long time. Vinny Del Negro, the N.C. State kid who also played and coached in the NBA for a long time, played over there too for the Italian club Benneton Treviso.

I was having a lot of fun, too. At that time, the summer before, I had met a model here in Kansas City named Serena and she moved to Fribourg to be with me. She was living with me there up until Christmas and she flew back to the States for the holidays, to spend time with her sister in California.

While she was gone, I went down to this American video store one night and I met this girl who would later become my wife. So, just like that, I called Serena and told her, don't come back. I had a lot of fun right away with the new girl and, frankly, I had gotten pretty tired of Serena anyway. She was a gold-digger and she was just along for the ride. She was like, "after the season you're going to buy a condo downtown in Kansas City and we're going to live there and I'm going to go to chiropractor's school." I'm thinking, "Who's going to pay for all this?" and I certainly knew the answer to that one. All she did was party the whole time in Switzerland when I was playing and practicing. She never had to lift a finger.

Billy Martin loved smoking hashish, which was prevalent in Europe at the time. He told me about this famous drug park in Bern, a place called Coker Park where you could go buy any kind of drugs you want and they would just leave you alone. I'm like, 'What?" But it was true. The authorities basically said that if there was one place for everyone to go to, and they just left them alone, that they wouldn't be anywhere else. It was sort of the government's way of containing the drug culture. Billy and I drove to the park because it was only like 15 minutes away, and oh, my

God, it was like walking into a scene from Land of the Zombies. There were people doing heroin like crazy, people walking around with needles sticking out of their arms and needles dangling from the vein in their necks. People were completely scabbed over and everybody would run up to you, wanting to sell you drugs. It was the craziest thing I had ever seen. You could buy anything you'd want in those parks. Zurich had a place like that too. It was called Needle Park, and it was famous. I went there once. It was amazing how many discarded dirty needles and baggies covered the grounds.

Billy would buy hashish to smoke but we would buy cocaine too, but it was like $300 for a gram of cocaine, which is nuts. It was ridiculously expense, and it was just junk. But we bought it anyway and our apartment wound up being a place where we would go party after games. We'd do a lot of drugs.

This was my team in Switzerland, where we won a league championship and played a lot of the big teams in Europe.

We knew a guy in Belgium named Richard Laurel and he could get us good cocaine any time. He got cocaine – and lots of it – for Darryl Dawkins all the time. He had been a big star in the NBA for years but now he was playing over in Milan, Italy, and man he loved his cocaine. Daryl played for Mike D'Antoni at the time. He came over and coached in the NBA a long time. But Richard Laurel would mail us cocaine all the time, big packages of it. We even drove all the way to Belgium one day, like 12 hours, just to party with him. We'd drive there, party all night, and then drive back.

That's when cocaine sort of became a regular thing for me. We always had a lot of cocaine around and that became our routine, that after every game we'd go back and party and I would do cocaine. Just relax and have fun, pretty much after every game. We would drink and have fun and that's what it was mostly about. I mean, the stuff we were getting, for $300 it wasn't much and it was maybe 20 percent pure. The stuff from Richard Laurel, that was way better.

I went back home for Christmas for a few days and this kind of shows how crazy it was starting to get for me. I bought an ounce of cocaine in Kansas City and then I went out and bought a bunch of Christmas cards. I smashed up the cocaine and put it inside the cards and mailed it back to Switzerland.

On New Year's Eve, they arrived in the mail to me in Switzerland and I remember me and Billy being so excited. Man, did we party that night. We got this cocaine from the States, and it worked, mailing it.

It worked so well I started having people in the States mail me smashed-up cocaine in envelopes all the time. No one ever noticed. Doing drugs like crazy, even having it mailed to me. It was a crazy time, no doubt about it.

19

Chapter

TROTTING AROUND THE GLOBE
YEAR AFTER YEAR

As much as I enjoyed Switzerland, you still had to go
where the money was, especially if it was a lot better. That happened in my fourth year over there, when I got an offer to play in
Belgium. It was a great offer, too, for $115,000. I was the highest-
paid player in Belgium, and this was the top team in Belgium.
That was the largest contract I had ever had in Europe. They really
wanted me because I had played well in Switzerland and was
coming off a championship season.

In Belgium, I played on a team with five Americans, because three of the guys had Belgian passports and weren't considered foreign players. Brian Shorter, who went to Pitt, was the other
American and we were a top team called Sun Air Oostende. We
had an American coach named Jim Parks, and he was good, but it
was a miserable situation.

The owner of the team owned Sun Air Airlines, and they
sponsored the team. But he didn't treat us like players, he treated
us like employees. He even said we had to work like every other
employee he had. He said we needed to show up at the gym at 8
and be home by 5, like every other regular employee. So we'd
practice for two hours in the morning, and then we'd stay there
and have lunch and we'd have to eat as a team every day. The we

135

would watch film together and then practice again for a couple of hours and go home at 5.

It was miserable. I hated it. I was hurting too, because my ankles were a mess. I started taking 3,200 milligrams of Ibuprofen every morning just to get through the day. I wasn't eating right when I took it either, and I wound up tearing up the lining in my stomach. I was a mess. I was living in a high-rise on the 32nd floor, but it was just nasty. There was garbage and dog crap everywhere and it was such a huge change from Switzerland, which was so super clean. Belgium was nasty dirty and I really hated it.

At that time, I contacted Didier Rose, the agent I knew over there, and I told him, please get me out of here. We negotiated a buyout, which was fair, and I hooked up with another team in France right after that. That was the first year that my wife and I had been together, and that was rough because that was the first time she had ever been away from home, first in Belgium and then in France.

I played in Berck-Sur-Mer, France, which is right there on the English Channel. I just played that year out. It was an interesting place, a small little village on the water. It wasn't much of a season, and it was strange being married and having to deal with Lara every day, especially since she hated being away from home. I was still feeling like crap, too. My stomach was still a mess and the team sent me to the doctor to get checked out. I couldn't keep food down and I had acid reflux something terrible. They wanted to check out my GI tract so they stuck a tube up me and had me stripped down naked on a table with two doctors and four nurses. It was embarrassing as hell, being there all naked and running back and forth to the toilet probably four or five times while they did all that stuff. I think they were having fun with the dumb-ass American on their table. My stomach was a mess, though. All that ibuprofen tore up my stomach. It's still an issue today.

As soon as the season ended, we went back to Switzerland. Lara hated the idea of moving to Belgium and France for a few months, but she dealt with it. But the next move was much bigger, and she didn't deal with that very well at all.

OLIMPIA 1-0   Página 30

Que pongan seis
extranjeros, yo me
arreglo con dos

Al Panathinaikos, que es una
sucursal de las Naciones Unidas,
el Olimpia de Segui le ganó con el
negro Wilson y el blanco Jadlow.

Victoriano está
para la prenda
En dos meses cumple
19 años. Juega como
en el patio de la casa.

Con espacio,
Zulberti la mata
Puso dos triples en el
debut. Los griegos lo
respetaron las canas.

My Olimpia team in Argentina was the best team I ever played on professionally. That's my teammate Mike Wilson on the left, and my coach, Horacio Segui.

The parade after we won the South American championship was the biggest gathering of people that I had ever seen. There were hundreds of thousands of people everywhere along the parade route.

20

Chapter

LIVING THE HIGH
LIFE IN ARGENTINA

Every summer, I'd go back to Switzerland, where my wife was from, and that really became home for me, more or less. I almost never came to the States. Fribourg was home for her, so it also become home to me after we got married. I met her at Christmastime, and we got married in June. My sister and my mother came over to the wedding, but my dad didn't. I re-signed to play at Fribourg again, but I didn't like it. It was a different coach and a different team and it just wasn't a good fit. I just played a short time there, and then I got a call from an agent named Fernando Bastide in Argentina. He asked me if I would be interested in coming to Argentina to play, and I said heck yeah. So I went to a place called Bahia Blanca, in 1994. Estudiantes was the name of the team, and my foreign teammate there was a Russian named Sergei Grishalev and he was a work of art.

It was an eye-opening experience. It was so hot there that they played all the games at 10 o'clock at night and the gyms were still hot. I loved playing there, loved the whole culture and everything about. I averaged 26.6 points and 8.6 rebounds a game that year.

Lara didn't stay with me there. I was there for five months by myself without her. And then she got mad when I didn't come back to Switzerland in the summer. I got offered $10,000 a month

Playing in Argentina was a lot like playing at Indiana because the fans were so intense about their teams. I made a lot of covers there, too.

to come play in a summer league in Montevideo, Uruguay in the offseason, which was a two-month thing. My agent down there, Fernando Bastide, warned me not to go because he didn't think it was the right place for me. He was right, because it was nuts over there. They played on outdoor courts with indoor/outdoor balls. But I bit the bullet because they were paying me $10,000 a month to do it, for a two-month league. But I broke my nose about a month into the season there and I left. It was a pretty rough situation.

Getting my nose fixed at the hospital in Uruguay was scary as hell. They wheeled me into a room to fix my nose and right there next to me, they're doing a surgery on a guy. His stomach is cut wide open and there's even a couple of other people getting worked on in the same operating room. Nothing was sterile and it was definitely less than pristine in there, not like you'd see in any operating room in the States. I went ahead with the surgery anyway and that was a huge mistake. They messed me up really bad, and I had to have it re-done a few months later when I came to the States. I was never so happy to get out of Uruguay.

*** *** ***

I really wanted to stay in Argentina after that, so in 1996, I signed with another good team called Quilmes in the first division in Marta Plata, which was a step up. Marta Plata was a resort city, and it was really nice. It was ten times better there than in Europe, both the quality of play and the fan support. The fans were crazy. Ricky Blanton, who had a great career at LSU, was my teammate there. So was Sepo Ginoboli, who was Manu's older brother. I played well there, too, and people noticed. I averaged 27 points a game there.

IN THEIR OWN WORDS

Fernando Bastide, South American sports agent

Back in the 1990s when Todd played, it wasn't nearly as easy to follow American players around the world as it is now. I first heard of Todd in the Blue Ribbon yearbook and I paid attention to him scoring in bunches in Switzerland, so I thought he would be a good fit in Argentina.

I got a deal for him with a top division team, Estudiantes, and they signed Todd and this big Russian. That was a real experience for Todd. He used to call me and tell me stories about him all the time. He'd call me and say "I give this guy towels and sheets and he doesn't use them. I give him deodorant and no. He doesn't even shower." That took some getting used to for him.

The biggest mistake Todd made with me was going to Uruguay to play during a summer. It's horrible there but he didn't listen to me. He got his nose broken there and one time I went up there to sign another player and Todd was playing in a game.

The setting was unbelievable. Small courts, right up against the walls, people pushing and shoving. Well, the game starts and a guy puts in his hand right in Todd's face. The refs? Nothing. They give Todd a technical. Then they give him another one. He sees me and says "Get me out of here." He always listened to me after that.

Todd was a really great player in Argentina. He could really score and rebound and he loved it there. Ricky Blanton, who played with him at Quilmes and had been a big star at LSU in college, said Todd got to know everyone in town and that he never paid for a meal. That was Todd.

Ricky said to me "Todd never pays for a dinner, a coffee or a coke. Each coin he gets, he keeps it." I laugh at that one all the time.

I came to the league in Argentina and I proved myself, so I had a chance to sign with Olimpia, which was a top team in Argentina based in Venado Tuerto. Andres Nocioni, who played with the Chicago Bulls, was a junior player on our team and the other American was Michael Wilson out of Pitt, and we had an incredible team. We had lots of guys who all bettered their positions around the world, and several players on our team were on the Argentina national team. Jorge Racca was the league MVP that year and he was a great player. To this day, a lot of people still call that the greatest team in the history of Argentina basketball.

That was the year that they had the very first South American Cup, and we won it. It was incredible. We won a game that was featured on Dateline NBC that was called the 'Brawl in Brazil." It was the first time in my life that I was actually scared and feared for my life leaving a game. We had won the championship – which was a huge, huge deal – and our guys were jumping on the scorer's table, showing off their jerseys and celebrating.

Well, a lot of these Brazilian fans, they got so mad that they started picking up their chairs and throwing them at us players. The game was played in Sao Paulo, Brazil, the capital, and those fans are wild. They just all ascended onto the court and it got way out of hand.

There were 10,000 people there and our coach, Juan, was on the floor bleeding. He got knocked out, and they had Mike cornered. Mike stood over Juan with a chair in each hand, fending off all these attackers. I took off running, trying to get away from the mob. And then when we were leaving, they were throwing these huge bricks at the bus, which were shattering all the windows on the bus.

We had a huge parade because we were champions of the whole country, so it was a huge deal. The parade was one of the

most incredible things I've ever seen. The national pride that came
with us winning that South American title was amazing and we
all become huge heroes overnight. If you can imagine the Macy's
parade in New York on Thanksgiving, that's what it was like. There
were hundreds of thousands of people, for miles and miles. It was
amazing.

We got all sorts of commercial deals, and there were huge
TV shows for us. We also went on to win the league championship
that year in a seven-game series against Atenas, which starred a
young kid named Fabricio Oberto. He played in the NBA with the
San Antonio Spurs, too.

Living in Venado Tuerto was awesome, and it really
felt like home to me. I met a lot of celebrities like Ricky Martin,
Inrique Iglesias and the soccer legend Diego Armando Maradona.
The women there were beautiful, and when Lara wasn't around I
spent time with someone different just about every night. It was a
great place to live because Venado Tuerto was all about the club,
Olimpia. We were all like rock stars in town. Everyone loved having us around. We would get invited to dinners and barbeques all
the time and on game nights, the town would basically shut down.
There would be 8,000 fans at every game and they were loud and
crazy. I loved it. The passion reminded me a lot of Indiana. It was
all about us.

I did lots of cocaine after games there. It was like $5 a
gram, maybe $10 at the most. The American and I went to lunch
every day at this same restaurant because it was part of our contract, and we met this guy who was a general in the Bolivian cartel.
He used to bring huge kilos of cocaine to my house.

I was scared to death of this guy. He would always tell
me, "If you need something taken care of, just let me know." He
was a scary, scary dude. He was bringing like 20 kilos of cocaine

and leaving it in my apartment and giving me a few ounces of cocaine for free, no questions asked. I just couldn't do that for long because I was scared to death something was going to happen.

My wife would come to visit in Argentina for a month or so at a time, but she wasn't over there very much. I had the life of Riley, doing whatever I wanted to do whenever I wanted to.

I did an enormous amount of cocaine that year. After every game, it was just a huge party, not only with my teammates but with players from the others teams as well. My first year at Olimpia, I remember one morning after we had been up all night partying, everyone had left and I thought I was having a heart attack.

So I walked over to the hospital and told them I thought I was having a heart attack. They said, "Why?" And I said it was because of cocaine. They did an EKG but they said I would be fine. I thought they would make a big deal out of it, but nobody said anything. The hospital didn't bill me or say anything. They just told me to go home. I thought for sure somebody would say something to me when I went back to practice, but it never came up.

*** *** ***

I re-signed with that team in 1997 after winning those two championships. During those two years, we all did a lot of commercials, and we were huge stars not only our town, but throughout Argentina. Everyone knew who we were. I averaged almost 30 points a game over there. I beat on everyone. When Ginoboli switched clubs, I beat him. Luis Scola, who played in the NBA a long time, he couldn't handle me either. It was a great decision for me to come to play in Argentina for those years, which was the best decision I ever made. I absolutely loved playing in Argentina and it was by far the favorite part of my career.

145

But the next year was when it turned into a disaster. The owner of the team was a guy named Roberto Cataldi and he also was president of the largest bank in Argentina, Banco Bid. When the government audited the bank they found hundreds of millions of dollars missing. So they arrested Cataldi and immediately froze the assets of everything, including the team, so nobody got paid and that ended up being that. The club wound up being millions of dollars in debt too, and this once-great club basically turned into nothing.

It was a bad situation for me because I had expected it to be so great. It was my largest contract ever, and we had a great team that was capable of winning more championships. And just like that, poof, it was over. I hired a lawyer to be paid my contract, and I won. They were ordered to pay me what they owed me and for a few months they did. Then a huge soccer club went under,

I really enjoyed playing for Deportivo Roca in Argentina, That's me in the white, driving to the basket against Fabricio Oberto on the left. He was young then, but later played in the NBA and was a really good player.

so the government changed the laws on how people had to get paid in those situations, so they stopped paying me. They still owe me more than $115,000. It's still an ongoing fight too, still going through the legal system, and it's a huge story down there in Argentina, even 20 years later. I'm glad I played there when I did, though. It was a blast. I absolutely love Argentina and the Argentine people.

*** *** ***

With the Argentina options gone, I went to Caracas, Venezuela to play for Panteras but that didn't last long because I feared for my life there. I had to escape from the country just to stay alive, it was that dangerous. One day, three other players were with me and we were just driving down a crowded six-lane highway when out of nowhere we got pulled over and surrounded by eight cops on motorcycles. They all pulled their guns out on us, just because we were in a nice car. They thought we were drug dealers. They made us get out of the car right in the middle of all that traffic and with guns pointed right at our heads, made us lay down on the ground. They frisked us with one hand while they kept the barrel of the gun right up against our heads. I could feel it on my head. It wasn't until one of my teammates, who was a Venezuelan national, told the cops we were basketball players. It took a while, but they finally let us go. I thought for sure I was going to die that day. They profiled us as drug dealers, not basketball players.

Just the night before at the hotel I stayed at, the clerk got shot and killed. I just couldn't stay there anymore. In the middle of the night, I snuck out of the hotel and went to the airport. I flew out and left the team there, right on the spot.

I went back to Argentina and signed with a team called Deportivo Roca, and that was my last year playing there. I loved Argentina, the people and the culture. I always felt like I was at home in Argentina, and I'm looking forward to going back there to visit someday.

I came back to the States and helped a minor-league team in Salina, and did that for two years. It was a USBL team called the Kansas Cagerz, but it wasn't much. I did it to help generate interest in the league in Salina, but it was only like $300 or $400 a week and that was it. I played and coached for the Cagerz. I was the general manager and the director of basketball operations for a team in the International Basketball Association called the Salina Rattlers, but that league didn't last very long.

We had two kids then, and when we came back to the States we had two more after that. But my basketball days were done. It was quite a run.

Argentina might be more known for soccer, but basketball was big when I was there, too, because our team was so good. I made lots of magazine covers.

21

Chapter

LIFE AFTER BASKETBALL
STARTS ROUGH BACK IN SALINA

When my basketball career was over, I wasn't ready for the next phase in my life. There were so many changes and, quite frankly, I didn't like any of them.

My wife and I decided to settle in Salina, Kansas, which had been home for me growing up. I took a job doing mortgages at a local bank, and that's how my post-basketball career was going to start. It wasn't the work that bothered me, because I knew there would always have to be some kind of career after basketball. I always did well in school and I felt like I had the smarts to do well in any kind of career.

It was every-day life after basketball that drove me nuts. When I was playing basketball all over the world, my wife and I rarely lived together for very long at the same time. She'd come visit for a few weeks or a month now and then, but we were never together for long stretches, and I had a lot of fun with other women when she was gone. A lot of fun.

Now, here we were in Kansas, living together all the time, and I hated it. I still wanted to live the life, to be out partying. I was used to being able to doing my own thing and then all of a sudden I couldn't. I was still out there enjoying the night life all the time, and then hanging out with other athletes still running around, but I still had to deal with her at home all the time, and all we did was fight. I can honestly say I didn't enjoy being at home with her. I loved being with my girls, but my wife and I, we fought all the time. It was an ugly time.

***   ***   ***

I was using a lot of cocaine at the time and had a couple of close calls with the law. I was very lucky I never got caught. When I was living in Salina, I routinely drove to Dallas to pick up large quantities of cocaine from a major dealer there. One night after driving to Dallas and returning at 2 a.m., I pulled into my grandmother's old house to hide a large amount of cocaine in an RV that I had owned and left parked there. I had just stashed six ounces of cocaine in the RV and as I was leaving the driveway, some DEA agents walked around the corner and stopped me in my car in the driveway.

I thought, "Oh, shit," as they showed me their badges, and I knew this wasn't going to be good. I had just stashed the large amount of cocaine in the RV and had a quarter of an ounce loose still in my shirt pocket I rolled down the window as they approached me and they ASKED ME WHERE MY UNCLE WAS. They thought HE was inside the house. They were looking for him, not me. I told them I didn't know where he was but would go inside the house to look. So I went inside my grandmother's house, but he was not there. I told them that at the front door and they just left.

I didn't get back in my car to leave because I could see them waiting outside in a car a little down the street. I was high as a kite and drunk at the time and had just stashed all that cocaine in the RV without getting caught. I dodged another bullet. God was

150

definitely with me and watching over me that night. How I did not get caught is beyond me. They apparently had no issues with me but wanted to talk with my uncle, who had had some issues with drugs and the police in the past. I was extremely lucky, but that night put the fear of God in me and I became super paranoid from that point on. From then on, I started digging holes in the ground and burying the cocaine there. I was lucky; that's all I can say.

***   ***   ***

In 1999 we built a house in Salina. and the two young-est girls came after that, in 1999 and 2001. My first brush with the law came then in Salina, but it was totally ridiculous. My wife and I got into an argument, and she walked by me and I kicked her in the butt, but not hard at all, and she called the cops. It was literally nothing. I was sitting down and just kicked her in the butt as she walked by. It wasn't that kind of fight.

But when the cops came, they said if they answer a call like this, that they have to take somebody in, so they took me in and arrested me on a domestic battery charge. That created a huge issue, because the issue of domestic violence was so prevalent at that time because of the O.J. Simpson case. I was done play-ing, but that really started a downward spiral for me because I had never been in trouble. I had a perfect image and then all of a sudden I got this, and I didn't really know how to handle it. It was a real shot at my reputation, and I hated it. It tore me up in every aspect of my life and created a sense of self-worthlessness. I didn't handle that situation well, and it created a larger mess for me in the way I reacted.

At that time, I was still acting crazy, drinking and partying and sleeping with all kinds of women, but it was a lot harder trying to keep it from her because we were supposed to be living in the same house. As it turns out, she was cheating as much as I was, so I guess it all evened out.

I was still finding my way, and I wasn't really doing a very good job of it, I guess. It was all about the next fun time, and I was always looking for something different. My life was definitely spinning out of control.

*** *** ***

We only stayed in Salina for a couple of years, and then I got a job with Glaxo Smith Kline selling pharmaceuticals and did really well with them. I won awards and was a top-three salesman in their company. But they eliminated the area I was working in, so they said I could live anywhere I wanted and they would transfer me, and that's when I picked Lawrence.

We moved there and built my dream house. It was seven bedrooms and four bathrooms and with a large arcade in it and a TV viewing room. It was a beautiful home that I truly loved. I worked for Glaxo for three years and it went well. Then I went to work for company called Biomet, and I was an orthopedic sales rep for them, doing sports medicine. As a sales rep for Biomet, I was responsible for all aspects of surgeon training and implementation of procedures in the operating room. I sold the implants that went into people and brought in all the instrumentation for surgery. I became a huge resource for the physicians with a lot of responsibility.

It was a good learning experience for me, and I did well. And it would be a good stepping stone for really doing well in that field a few years later.

22

Chapter

THE RESTAURANT LIFE IN KANSAS CITY
AND SO MUCH MORE

One of the best things I ever did was open a restaurant in Kansas City, for a lot of reasons, really. It gave me the outlet I needed, but there was also a great sense of accomplishment because it was a great place and everybody loved it.

It was called SoRedux and it was the only four-star restaurant in Kansas City. I also had the only four-star chef in Kansas City. That was fun. It was in 2006 when it opened, and it was so classy. Great food, great wines, perfect setting. It was a big hit right from the get-go. SoRedux was all about the art of conversation and a great culinary experience. We paired five-to-seven plates with five-to-seven wines, and dinner there was truly an event. Dinner usually lasted three hours and we had a very high-end clientele. The food and wine were incredible, as was the atmosphere in the historic Columbus Park section of Kansas City. We sat right on the edge of downtown and at night we had a picturesque view of the skyline of downtown Kansas City.

We were profitable within the first couple of months, which is unheard of in the restaurant business. We had a great location in Little Italy in Kansas City, in this great, old building. It was Pretty Boy Floyd's old hangout and all the old Italians would come by and tell us stories all the time. I was sure it was haunted, that old building. Doors would open and close all the time, and those old cellars, I swear the walls could talk.

It was open for three years and did really well. I was very hand's on when it opened. It could have been great. I did it all myself. I got the liquor license myself, got it rezoned myself. I learned a lot about that business and got it open and it was great, right from the start. Very few restaurants survive and thrive and make money, but you've got to be there 24/7 to really make it work.

It was fine dining and it was a great place to entertain. It served that purpose for me too. I brought a lot of my doctors in there and had lots of meetings and talks there too. I loved being there and working the room, saying hello to people and making sure everyone was having a great time. We had great food and a great wine selection and it was crowded all the time.

It was also a great place for me to have fun. I did a lot of cocaine there and drank a lot there. It was a place for me to escape, with all the problems I was having in my marriage. I would stay there all night a lot of times. I liked being at the restaurant a lot more than I liked being at home.

It went really well until the people that worked there started stealing from me all the time. I couldn't be there as much as I needed to be, because my orthopedics business was getting so big. I had a problem with the chef, Pete Peterman. He just had a dirty character and he thought he was bigger than life. He was a great chef, but he was horrible dealing with people and he embarrassed me all the time.

One night we had a group of prominent attorneys come in and they spent a fortune. But they had arrived late and at the end of the meal the chef Peterman comes out and says "Are you the group that came in late? Don't ever come in here again." He had that type of character, Pete Peterman. And he was stealing from me like crazy. He was buying stuff at Costco for the restaurant, but then he would buy bikes and furniture and stuff and charge it to the restaurant. He was buying food – high-end food – and selling it to other restaurants and keeping the cash.

He ripped me off every way he could. When I wasn't around at night, he would say there were a lot of cancelled reservations, but all he was doing was pocketing the cash and not telling me about it. I even caught him doing it one time. I gave my friends cash to go in there, and the next day he'd tell me they cancelled. He'd lie right to my face.

I just couldn't do it anymore, so I decided to close the restaurant. I had some friends help me and we just emptied the place out. Took all the wine and everything, everything that I had paid for, and just padlocked the door. We took everything that I had bought. We had old New York-style rollers and I padlocked all of them around the building and put a "Closed" sign on it.

The Kansas City Star found out about it because we were the only 4-star restaurant and they wrote it like it was a hostile takeover, but that wasn't it. I had just had enough with Pete. I paid for all his housing, everything, so it was a mess. I held on to the building for six more months myself, but I could never re-open it because we had done some things to skate around the building codes when we opened and it would have costs thousands to fix it up properly.

Pete held that against me that he'd report me if I tried to re-open. I would have loved to re-open it with somebody else, but that wasn't really an option.

He just never saw the big picture, and it was too bad. We both could have made a fortune. I was worn out by that whole experience. So when I closed it, I was still making six figures with the orthopedics, so it wasn't like I was hurting. But it's one of my big regrets, having to close it. I really loved that business. I used it a lot to get business with doctors too, entertaining them at the restaurant. I absolutely loved the restaurant business. I would do it again if it was the right situation.

*** *** ***

I was doing everything right with work in those days, but I was still partying real hard and no one even knew it. My home life was horrible, so Lara and I got divorced in 2007, during the restaurant time. It took three years to get divorced. It wasn't good. It was all about money. I walked away from everything in the house. It was a nightmare. Lara had the life of Riley. I worked and she stayed home, and I even took care of the kids most of the time. At that time, Lara was good at three things, and three things only. She was good at going to the gym every day; she was good at doing lots of cocaine, even when she was pregnant with our last two daughters; and she was good at dropping her pants for all sorts of other guys.

It was just time. The first ten years we were married, we didn't even really live together when I was playing. After I retired from basketball and we moved to Salina, that was the first time we ever actually lived together for a long stretch of time. When we got married, I had only known her for six months. It was the first of many of my rash decisions that came back to bite me. I was the one who ran the kids all around, and she just went to the gym and had her fun and she had some boyfriends on the side. It all came to an end when I found out she was cheating, but I had no feelings for her anymore, and I hadn't for years.

I was just ready to move on. I was miserable.

***   ***   ***

I was doing a lot of drinking and drugs when I owned the restaurant. One time I had a loaner car from BMW because my car was in the shop. It had like two miles on it when they gave it to me. When I left the restaurant, I was so high that I hit the median and I broke both rims, both tires, and I scraped the side. I was such a mess with all the drugs in me that I just sat there trying to figure out what to do.

I had a quarter ounce of blow on me at the time and just sat there in the car sniffing it like there was no tomorrow. That Monday I called the BMW dealership and told them where their car was and they went and picked it up and were shocked to see the state it was in. I had done $10,000 in damage to a new car and just paid for the repairs out of my pocket, That became a really expensive night of partying.

Another time I left the restaurant all messed up on Interstate-70 and I blew out a tire in my BMW. As I was waiting for BMW Assist to drive out to me to fix my tire, a cop pulled up. I had already went into an adjoining field and threw out the cocaine I had just in case. When the cop arrived. I just cracked the window and the cop asked me what I was doing there. I told him I was waiting for help to fix the tire and he just shook his head and walked away. Another bullet dodged.

Once in Lake of the Ozarks at 4 in the morning, I was drunk and high and I was going 70 miles per hour in a 30. I got pulled over but all he did was write me a speeding ticket and then he let me go.

I always avoided getting DUIs, and I guess I was pretty lucky. That wouldn't last forever.

***   ***   ***

One of the biggest problems with being messed up all the time is that it's easy to make bad decisions. I made plenty, but nothing was bigger than the mistake I made with a crazy, heartless woman named Nancy Dodik.

That nightmare began on Sept. 28, 2009. It was my daughter Kiara's eighth birthday and as part of her celebration she wanted a limo ride from school to my home in Overland Park. Nancy was the mother of one of Kiara's friends who came along with us on the limo ride and I met her that day.

And then the bad decisions started promptly. We spent a lot of time together, and there was a lot of drinking involved. Everybody who knew her kept telling me to stay away from her, that she was a crazy gold-digger and was just trying to get her hooks in me.

They were right. I was foolish enough to marry her after only a few months of dating. She got pregnant and later had our daughter Camryn, but it's been nothing but trouble ever since with her. I wish I would have listened to my friends on that one. She basically destroyed my life.

That marriage was just a joke. It's the perfect example of why you don't do things impulsively. Getting married three months after we met was just insanity. People were warning me about her left and right, but I'm sure all the cocaine in my brain was affecting my ability to make good decisions then. And to think, all the bad, crazy stuff that went on during those three months with her, and I married her anyway. What the hell was I thinking? That's stupidity. I was warned so many times by people, and I saw her crazy family in action.

I was Captain Save-A-Ho, I suppose.

158

23

Chapter

INTO THE OPERATING ROOM
AS A STAR IN BUSINESS

For a lot of professional athletes, finding a career after basketball is difficult. Many of us knew nothing but basketball for a lot of our lives, and when it ends, finding something else to do isn't easy.

Thankfully, that wasn't my problem. I certainly struggled with "life" after basketball, but I didn't have any trouble making a good living. The best job I had was with Zimmer, where I spent seven years helping surgeons do total joint reconstruction and trauma cases. I was very successful and made a lot of money. I made more every year doing that than I did playing basketball overseas. That's how good I was at what I did.

The money was great in that field, at least for most of my career. Some surgeries, I'd be there an hour and make $5,000. Others might only pay $700 or $800, but I could do seven or eight of those a day. My doctors loved me, because I could literally talk them through all the surgeries. I knew it all like the back of my hand.

Because I did so well, they got me involved with joint reconstructions. I learned all sorts of stuff and made really good money. My partner was making double what the surgeons were making. It was an extremely lucrative field. Once I got fully engrained in orthopedics, that's when I wanted to do the restaurant too. It was a good time. I was working like crazy, but it was worth it because I was making a lot of money.

But for as much money as I was making, I was still living month to month. I would make between $15,000 and $25,000 a month cash and I'd still blow through it all partying.

I worked for Zimmer for seven years, until Aug. 18, 2012. That was my last day of work and the ending was very bitter. They took me from a 1099 employee to a W-2, and they put me on salary. They took away all my joint business, which is where I made all my money, and they just wanted to make me a trauma guy. It was a massive pay cut. They took my income to about a third of what I was making and what I had built up over nine years. And it was like, take it or leave it. There were new bosses, and the corporate mentality changed completely. They really treated people poorly, so it just kind of ended.

And since I had a non-compete clause, there was nowhere else for me to go in that business. They threatened me, because I had other opportunities, but I wasn't in a position to fight them. They were going to sue me if I took my doctors with me and went somewhere else. It became kind of a nightmare.

When the commission structure changed, it just ruined it for me. It was typical corporate greed, it just killed me. I had 11 years in that business, and when they made me salary, it was like a third of what I was making. I was the one who built up the whole business and they didn't care.

During those times I used a lot of cocaine and alcohol but never let it interfere with my work. I would pick and choose when I would allow myself to use. Very few people knew that I did cocaine, but one of them was one of the doctors I worked with all the time. Yes, even surgeons like to party. And some of them party pretty hard, but they were a lot like me, picking and choosing their spots carefully. We would go out for drinks and they would talk about doing coke or smoking pot. I did cocaine with one of them on several occasions.

I was doing a lot of partying then, because I had money to burn. I was hanging around a lot with Tony Richardson, who used to play for the Kansas City Chiefs. A lot of nights Tony and I would go to this club called Mosaic in Kansas City. It was a bottle club, and there were some nights we'd spent $8,000 or $10,000 a night. Some nights we'd have 10 or 20 bottles on the table and I'd ask Tony why he was ordering more, and he'd say he liked the sparklers on the bottle when they brought it out.

That was typical. It was just insanity and there was always cocaine around, and I did a lot of it, but never with Tony. I heard Tony liked the party favors too, but I never did cocaine with him, just a whole lot of drinking. We just drank together. I think both of us were embarrassed, being model athletes. You keep the cocaine use private, I guess, because you didn't want anybody to know.

I had my other running mate I did cocaine with. I'd get an ounce of cocaine and I'd call him and he'd come over and stay for a couple of days. He'd tell his wife I was depressed and he'd come stay. It was a revolving door of women. We'd go on the internet and call them over. They'd be there and party with us. They'd steal stuff left and right and take our drugs but we didn't care. It was that out of control.

Me and Tony, some night there would be ten women there. There was a lot of nudity, and a lot of stuff going on behind closed doors. I always had cocaine with me, and now I know Tony did too. We were just total out of control over the top partying. Then we'd try to top it the next day.

IN THEIR OWN WORDS

Jamie Carpenter, Todd's girlfriend

I met Todd in January of 2012 through a Kansas City matchmaker we had both hired. We dated for about seven weeks but it was clear to me there were some issues going on with him and it wasn't going to work. I just had a different life from the one he had at that time.

We would talk now and then and stay in touch and in the summer of 2013 we reconnected but it was really hard. Todd was not in the best place then. He was a mess from his car accident and he just had a lot of bad things going on. I tried to be there for him, drive him around, help him with his girls. I got to spend a lot of time with his two girls, and they were a real pleasure to be around. I really enjoyed that.

But at that time I felt like he was never going to change, and we went in and out of each other's lives quite a bit. It was extremely difficult to be around him. You could see all his good points, but it was just difficult for them to all come to the surface. It wasn't until December, the month he went to jail, that he finally told me about all his drug use.

I can't say I was surprised because I had witnessed a lot of his bizarre behavior before during those times. But I also saw a good man inside of him and I was hoping someday those good things would start to shine through.

***   ***   ***

It's one thing to be partying it up all the time and trolling through women one right after another, but even through all those crazy times, I still wanted to see if I could find the perfect girl. I paid a fee to be part of a high-end matchmaking service in Kansas City and I was introduced to a few nice women.

None of them stuck. That was always on me, of course, because I was partying too hard to really care all that much.

I met this one girl in early 2012 and we went out for a few weeks. But it didn't work and she kicked me to the curb. How much did I care at the time? Not one bit.

Her name? Jamie Carpenter.

She would come back into my life later. Thank you, God.

24
Chapter

THE CAR CRASH
THAT CHANGED EVERYTHING

In November of 2011, Tony Richardson and I went down
to San Antonio to go on a hunting trip with Priest Holmes, the former Chiefs running back who had become a good friend of mine
and lived down there now. Rick Rodriguez, a big-time real estate
mogul in San Antonio and one of Priest's financial partners, also
was with us. We went hunting there at a place called Joshua Creek
Ranch and spent a couple days there. It was an incredible place,
just gorgeous. We had a lot of fun.

Afterward we went to Priest's nightclub, Area 31, and had
a great time. I ran into Manu Ginoboli there after a Spurs game and
he's like, "Todd, what are you doing here?" Manu was a star with
the San Antonio Spurs and he's won a lot of NBA titles. He's from
Argentina and I knew him well from when I played down there.

Not long after, when we got home, Tony and I were on the
highway in my brand new BMW 750IL Active Hybrid with twin
turbos, and it was a very rare car to have at the time. It was my
dream car and I finally had it. I had it for about a month and I just
loved it. It cost me $130,000 and it was loaded with every gadget
imaginable. We were on the highway where there was a lot of
construction, and they had taken three lanes down to one. We were
completely stopped, but this tractor-trailer didn't stop and ran right

into the back of our car going 50 miles an hour. I thought a bomb had exploded, the contact was so violent. He hit us so hard it threw us across the car. I opened my eyes and turned to Tony and he said "I can't move my back." The truck driver who hit us knocked on our window to make sure we were OK. We were alive, but both of us were banged up really bad.

The impact was huge. My headrest got bent really bad from my head hitting off of it. I had a whole host of problems after that. I had a severe concussion, I hurt my neck really bad and my back got messed up too. I had a few concussions before, but this was way worse than anything I had ever had. It was so hard for me to work, because my head was messed up. I would forget things all the time. I would spend an hour looking for my keys, and they would be in my hand the whole time. I would never know if I had taken my medicine or not, because I couldn't remember. I

I went on a hunting trip with former Kansas City Chiefs players Priest Holmes and Tony Richardson and a few others in Texas.

would forget things people would say to me because my short-term memory was just gone.

At work, I would go into surgeries and I would have two or three suites going. For years, the doctors I worked with would leave me in the room and say "Make sure the resident does this right." I would walk him through the surgery and tell him what to do, that's how well I knew everything. But after the accident, I couldn't remember everything. I had done a thousand of those surgeries, and then I was having to read a manual before I went into the operating room. I couldn't remember anything. I couldn't comprehend it, or process it.

I was a mess physically, too. I had issues with two disks in my neck and issues with the concussion, of course. I had tinnitus, and the ringing in my ears drove me crazy. I had PTSD really bad, too, I was scared to drive my car. Sometimes I'd just sit behind the wheel shaking, it was that bad.

And my brain was mush. I did what I did, basically with a cumulative of five years of medical schooling for any sports surgery to any total joint replacement. I could do any kind of revision, too. Then I was all trauma trained, too, and I could do it all in an operating room.

And then I couldn't even remember my last name.

I had an attorney in downtown Kansas City named Shawn Foster and we filed suit against the driver and the trucking company and there were several cases filed. I really needed the money after a while and didn't want to lose it. I went to one of those services that advances you on a settlement, but they rip you off so crazy. So I borrowed $30,000, which was $90,000 in payback once it was all said and done. But I needed the money – not for drugs or anything, just for paying bills – so I did it.

When Zimmer cut my salary back so far, it was time for us

to part ways. They would say they fired me, but I was leaving anyway. I was definitely having problems working but that didn't have anything to do with how they restructured my salary. They were doing that to everybody. And messed up or not, I wasn't going to put up with that. So I left.

But from that day on, I was so angry. I was living this big party life and now I couldn't even make my car payment. I couldn't afford my lifestyle anymore because I was living paycheck to paycheck. Now I couldn't afford anything because they had said take it or leave it. When we parted ways in August of 2012, that night I bought some drugs and grabbed a chick and it started the party. I didn't care, so it become an every night thing.

The accident exacerbated my problems, no doubt about it. Before the accident, I used a lot of cocaine to mellow out my drinking. I know it sounds crazy, but that's when I fell apart, after the accident, because I couldn't afford coke anymore when I wasn't working. I was just drinking then, But when I drank and I was on 12 medications, I was crazy. I was drinking all the time and I was a mess.

Because I wasn't working and I was in so much pain, I was always drinking. It was a constant party at my house. There would be girls coming and going and it was insane. I was drinking twice as hard. I didn't need the cocaine anyway because I was already taking so many drugs from the car accident. I was on hydrocodone for my ankle, Clonazepam for anxiety, two different types of anti-depressants, medication for Alzheimer's to restore my brain receptors, Ridilan for my ADHH, Ambien and Trazadone to sleep and I had never take any medication in all my life except for the hydrocodone for my ankles, which I've taken since they were fused. I was a walking pharmacy.

I was also a walking liquor store. I would buy a 1.75-liter

bottle of vodka just about every day. I think the concussion had a lot to do with that, because I certainly wasn't thinking well. I also didn't care. The concussion from the accident, that was not my first concussion. I had at least four other concussions that were either sports related or car-wreck related. It might have been an accumulation of things, but this one really put me over the top mentally.

My neck was a mess, too. I had 15 or so injections into my spine and that was always scary, going through that. It would alleviate the pain, but it wouldn't last for long.

None of the physical stuff compared to the depth of the depression though. After basketball ends, you have to rely on other things. I always did well in school and my mind was always good, but after the accident, I had all sorts of memory issues where people would tell me all the time that they told me things and I didn't remember. It would make me angry a lot that people would say it, but there were others who said they were there and they remembered it, but I didn't.

Mentally, I got to a place where I didn't care to live. The depression came real quick after the accident because I just couldn't work. I couldn't remember anything I would read about a case.

I took a lot of medicine to try to help restore the brain receptors again. I was taking all sorts of other medicines as well for depression and anxiety and add that to the 1.75 liters of Three Olives grape vodka and I was a mess. Physically, I felt terrible and mentally I was even worse.

So drinking was my outlet. With Priest and Tony, I'm thinking I'm back in the game when I'm partying with them. The parties and the women were crazy. It'd be me and Tony and 10 different women. What went on was nuts. Lots of cocaine and "skiing the slopes," like we called it, snorting cocaine off of women's breasts and nipples and the rest of their bodies. I'm 40-something years old, acting like I'm 20 again, and I'm acting so childish. It was all about the adrenaline rush.

It's hard to say no to fun. The adrenaline rush was constant, and I craved and needed something new every hour. I got really out of hand. It'd be seven or eight in the morning, and Tony is like, "Come on over." There would already be girls and drugs and it didn't matter the time of day. Tony and I had a lot of fun. And it was every day. He lived a mile from me and we were always together, all hours of the day. We were always drinking. And if we went out to dinner, it was always expensive wine and women around. It was always out of control with me and Tony.

After the accident, I had to write down everything I had to do. I had to make lists just to get through the day. I still have issues with taking medication. Two minutes later, I don't remember if I took it or not. I used to have a great memory, and now I try to force myself to not rely on writing notes all the time.

After the accident, I think it had to be a factor with work and what they thought of me. I never told them about the accident. I had help, someone I was showing how to do things, to help me after that accident. When they let me go, they said I was incapable of doing my duties, but I was still capable. All the surgeons revolted, too. They told Zimmer that if they sent in any other rep besides me, they wouldn't use their product. It became a mess. They were so mad they took me away from them, because I knew what they were doing. A lot of the surgeoons were my friends though, too. I partied with some of them too.

After that, I started drinking and partying a lot because I wasn't working. That was all. I had no direction. I didn't do anything. I drew unemployment for a while, but that's when things really started to fall apart. I was living by myself then, so I really didn't have anyone to answer to.

It was everything hitting me all at once. I didn't have money, I was depressed as hell and even trying to find a new job was hard, because I was so depressed I wanted to sleep all day. I had no energy or motivation to do anything.

Life sucked.

25

Chapter

OFF TO THE HOSPITAL TO DIE,
AND STILL NOT SLOWING DOWN

It was September 28, 2013 and I was lying down next to my youngest daughter, Camryn. We had a big birthday party for my daughter Kiara that day, and I had been drinking all day. I put Camryn to bed and I couldn't stop coughing. I went into the bathroom and I started coughing up blood. I didn't think that much about it and I went back to bed. I don't know what came over me, but I told myself if I go to sleep I'm not going to wake up. I just had this feeling that I wouldn't get through the night.

I kept vomiting blood and I knew something wasn't right. At midnight I called my sister, and by the time she picked me up and I walked into the hospital, I could barely breathe. She lived right near me in Overland Park and the hospital was only five minutes away. Taking a breath was almost impossible, so they admitted me right away. My lungs were completely full of infection. The left lung was 100 percent full and the right one was 90 percent full. I was that close to not being able to breathe at all. They admitted me to the Intensive Care Unit right away because I was deteriorating quickly. They wanted to intubate me but I refused. I wouldn't let them do it, because I was really worried that I wouldn't wake up. I sat on the edge of the bed for two days sitting up, because I couldn't lay down and still breathe.

I was in the ICU for ten days and in the hospital for over two weeks with pneumonia. I was about as close to dying as I had ever been. I was released and headed for home with a breathing unit and oxygen. I am sure my drinking and use of prescription drugs had a lot to do with it. I was in a very dark place in life, but I came through it somehow.

They found out I had staph and strep pneumonia and a lot of older people don't get over that. It was that bad. Then I also got a bacterial infection and I was in the bathroom the whole time. After the ICU and the other five days, I told them I was done. I told them I was leaving but they said if I could take a lap OK, I could go home. I told them I was going home regardless. I got a breathing machine and all my medications and went home.

I was really close to death, from what they told me. I got home and rested, but a week later a friend of mine who owns a restaurant on Southwest Boulevard called me. I'd drive around with him and do things, and right there, I was already drinking again. A week later, that's how crazy I was.

My drinking was so out of control because I had basically said to hell with everything. I would drink hard every single day, and it was the same routine. I would never buy a case at a time or anything. I would go every day to the liquor store, get a big bottle of vodka for $18 or $20 at Lionsgate Liquor Store in Leawood, Kansas. I even had their number in my phone. I'd get my Three Olives grape vodka and my Red Bull and I was off and running.

I would drink about three-quarters of a bottle every day. I got a bad case of "to hell with its" and I would start drinking as soon as I got up. Or at least by noon time, for sure. At the time, I'm still seeing all sorts of doctors, and seeing psychiatrists to help me with the depression, I was seeing a speech pathologist to help with my memory, and I was doing a lot of brain games. I was also seeing a pain management specialist for the disks in my neck. They'd stick a needle down there to keep it numb.

The mental stuff never really got better. I would only see the specialist to get the medications I needed. Anxiety, depression, sleep aids, I had medication for all of it. I had people tell me that when I would sleep at night, that I would quit breathing for long stretches. My body was a mess.

I could never even get in my car without having a drink with me. It was constant and all the time with me. One judge told me one time that if someone gets caught four times with a DUI that they probably should have been caught 4,000 times. That sounded like me.

My first DUI was in May of 2013. I remember I was driving and I dropped my phone. When I grabbed it, I veered over twice and someone called on me. I was going 100 miles per hour then too. I got arrested, paid $500 and got out, and when I got back in my car my drink was still there so I drank it on the way home. I had a good attorney, so it sort of went away. It was on my record, but there was no fine or probation or anything. Moving on, unharmed.

My second DUI, I met a friend at a sushi restaurant . This was in Overland Park and after I left, the police pulled me over and it was the same routine. They asked me if I had been drinking and would I take a breathalyzer. I said no, so they arrested me and towed my car. It was pretty clear I had no intention of changing my behavior. Getting off easy didn't have a bearing on me either, really. A normal person, after the first DUI, would make some changes, but for me it didn't even register. I couldn't hold a thought anyway. Those DUIs, they were no deterrent.

. Neither was being sick. I went to the hospital on Sept. 28 and spent nearly a month there. But by Halloween, I was drinking

175

up a storm already. In November, I had a girl over and I was so drunk that I sent out a big group e-mail that I was going to disappear and be done with life. One of my doctor friends and a scrub tech from KU called the cops because they thought it was a suicide note. I don't know, maybe it was. They came and I went out of my mind with the cops, and they took me to the KU hospital.

I had guns in my house and I could have been thinking about it. She told them where my guns were and the police took them all. They took me to the psych ward at KU and made me spend the night. I said it was all a misunderstanding with the e-mail and they finally let me go a day later. But my doctor friend who had called the cops, he was really upset that they let me go. He knew I was right on the edge and he was scared for my life.

He cared about my life a lot more than I did.

***　　***　　***

After that incident with the cops and my guns, my parents came and got me and they got all over me for my drinking, but I told them it was more the depression than the drinking. They wanted me to go to this place called Valley Hope, and they wouldn't leave me alone until I agreed to go. It was a rehab place and I went there for ten days and it didn't do anything. I went right back to drinking as soon as I came home. It was that fast. I had zero interest in stopping drinking.

I had no intention of changing anything. I never experienced the shakes or tremors or getting sick at rehab like a lot of people do. They put me on no medication and it did nothing for me. As soon as I got out, I went right back to drinking and taking all my medicines again.

I butted heads with the people at Valley Hope. They thought if you had one drink you're an alcoholic. We fought about my prescription medication stuff too, because for me that was a quality of life thing because my ankles were so bad. I had 12 surgeries on my ankles, had one fused twice. I needed medication to get through the day for that. They never understood my need for painkillers.

26

Chapter

MY TWO DUIs
ON THE SAME DAY

If you've ever wondered if it's possible to get two DUIs in the same day, I can tell you that it is. I did it, and I'm sad to say it's actually pretty easy to do.

It happened for me on Dec. 11, 2013, and it will go down as a defining day in my life. It defines me now, because it was the day that was the starting point for turning my life around.

But it was also a day that defined me as a worthless, non-caring drunk who had such problems that I didn't think twice about driving down the highway at 121 miles per hour with my 2-year-old daughter in the car with me.

A hundred twenty-one miles an hour, with a 2-year-old … and drunk on my ass. That's about as bad as it gets.

And that's just the end of my day.

The start of my day? That started the day before, of course, on Dec. 10, I had a girlfriend of mine with me, and we sat home and drank all day. She was working at a bar that night called Tanner's, so I took her to work, and then I stayed around there, drinking and eating until about 8 o'clock.

I was really drunk, and I guess I was being pretty obnoxious there because they threw me out.

I was just drinking away and I talked to Priest on the

phone for quite a while. This guy sitting next to me was asking me about the food there and I told him it sucked, that he shouldn't eat it, it was so bad. Well, the manager heard me and he was pissed, so he told me to leave. I was pretty pissed too. My bill was like $50, but I threw a $100 bill at him and told him to shove it.

I drove home – uneventfully – and had a few more drinks and I went to bed nice and early, like 10 o'clock. I was sound

asleep and at 2 o'clock in the morning I get a call from my friend at Tanner's, saying she needed a ride home. I told her I'd be there to get her, but first I went to Wal-Mart and bought some vodka. I got to the parking lot at Tanner's but there was no one in it. My friend isn't anywhere, and

that really pissed me off.

So I started driving home from Tanner's, and just like that, the cop lights me up, like he was waiting for me. I said "Why did you pull me over?" He said I touched the yellow line a few times. I still think somebody set me up. He asked me if I had been drinking, and I told him I had been earlier. He asked me if I would take a test and I told him no, and that was that.

He took me in to Overland Park to arrest me and I was able to call my sister when I got there. They did the paperwork and I was in and out that fast. They arrested me for a DUI, I signed the paperwork and they let me go. It was like getting a ticket, that's it. I bet I wasn't there more than an hour or so. They don't put you in a cell or anything. I just filled out some paperwork, signed it and left.

The first DUI of the day was in the books.

My sister got me and took me to my car and I went home. I got back to my house and that woman was there and she's yelling at me, like "Where the hell have you been?" I'm like "Where were you?" So we fought and fought, and I told her to get the hell out of my house. I threw her out. She tried stealing my watches on the way out, so I locked the house up and went to bed for a few hours.

I woke up about 10 in the morning and I went straight to the liquor store to buy more vodka, and by 11 in the morning I was back at my house drinking. Yeah, I can do that math, and there I was drinking away, less than eight hours after I had been arrested for a DUI.

I drank until about 2 o'clock in the afternoon, and then I drove to Lawrence to go get my oldest daughter at her apartment. I needed to go to day care to pick up my 2-year-old daughter, and I knew there would be no way they would let me pick her up, so I needed my daughter to do it. She went into day care and picked up my 2-year-old daughter and we left.

We got back to my daughter's apartment and she said, "Dad, don't leave" because she knew I was drinking. She wanted me to hang out there for a while, but I didn't want to do it. I told her no and I left with Camryn.

So I get out on the highway to go home and going the speed limit the whole way. I am driving on a suspended license as it is and I've been drinking, so I'm very aware of the fact that I do not want to get pulled over. I'm going 70 the whole way, but to be honest, that's mostly because these three cars in front of me are going too slow and they are in my way. I couldn't get past them and I was getting pissed.

They finally moved out of my way, and I saw my opening and floored it, I went from 70 to 120 miles per hour just like that, in a matter of seconds.

181

The cop, he was right there as soon as I hit it.

So his lights come on and I pull over right away. He asked me if I was drinking, and I said no, which was a lie, of course, although it had been an hour or two so since I had. I really didn't think I was drunk at the time but I took two Clonazepam for anxiety and I had never done that before, taking those and drinking at the same time. I was impaired for sure, because I had been drinking from 10 until about 2 in the afternoon. This was like 5 in the afternoon and they've got me. He asked me to blow, but I told him no, so in we go.

The Johnson County sheriffs took me in, and they took my daughter. They called my sister to get my daughter and she sat there with Camryn until her mom came.

Was I even worried about driving like that with my daughter in the car? To be honest, no I wasn't, not at the time. I never thought for a second about the stupidity of driving drunk with my 2-year-old in the car. Frankly, my worry then was more that I had a suspended license and I couldn't get pulled over no matter what, whether I was drinking or not. My mind just wasn't working right at the time. I think because of the concussion from my car accident, that nothing really registered mentally with me. Throughout my life I never repeated mistakes, but now I didn't have the cognitive ability to even correctly think about what I was doing. The accident magnified everything.

They took me to jail and it took forever. I knew nothing different about the system and I thought I could walk right out again, just like I had in the morning and the two previous times. But this time they told me no, that there would be no bond, and I really got mad. Soon after that, they got a warrant so they could take blood from me, since I refused to take a breathalyzer. They took me to the hospital to take my blood, and then I went to the holding area in the jail. My blood-alcohol level was 0.11, which was over the limit by three-hundredths, so I went to jail. It didn't seem real.

Once they brought me back from the blood test, they put me in a cell and then I didn't see anybody for a while. I fell asleep, and, to be honest, I really didn't care. A few hours later the clock struck midnight and Dec. 11 was over.

Two DUIs in one day … and it really wasn't hard to do at all.

27

Chapter

GOING INTO JAIL
FOR THE FIRST TIME

The first three DUIs I had in the previous six months, all I had to do was fill out some paperwork and within an hour or so I was on my way out the door. In a matter of hours, I was back home … drink in hand.

This fourth DUI though, that wasn't going to happen. They knew all about the DUI that I had earlier that day, and that was one thing. But having my 2-year-old in the car, too, well that really got them angry. Child endangerment charges were coming along, too. I wasn't going anywhere.

I just went to sleep in this tiny 8-by-8 cell in Olathe, Kansas, with one tiny little window. This was considered pre-class holding, and I was put in orange jail garb and flip-flops. I had to stay in that cell for nearly 23 hours a day. We were only let out of our cells three times a day for 30 minutes at a time, and it was a mad dash for one of the three phones. Since there were 50 guys there in holding, the chances of actually being able to make a call were pretty slim.

I couldn't remember anybody's phone numbers. I asked a guard if they could look up my sister's number and they did, but she refused to take my call. Every time I called, it just rang and rang. With the way cell phones work anymore, I didn't know anybody else's phone number, so I just sat there day after day. I asked them when I was getting out, and they had a very simple answer to that one:

"You're not."

What was really real was getting the jail garb, the two blankets, and these ugly orange Crocs and that was it. I got strip-searched, which was humiliating as hell. And when they walk you into that pod with 50 people staring at you, well it was crazy and frightening. I was intimidated by the whole experience and I felt so helpless. It overwhelmed me, that's for sure, just facing the reality that I was in jail and had no idea how to get out.

It was hard to realize I was going to be in jail for a while when I found out there was going to be no bond and I had to stay locked up. I finally had my arraignment in Olathe, and they went on and on about how I was a danger to society and I shouldn't be allowed to be let out. They finally set the bond at $100,000, which is unheard of for a DUI case. But there was a child endangerment charge, too, because my daughter was in the car, so that's why it got so high, but even that amount was abnormally high. There was no way I could pay to get myself out, and they weren't going to let that happen anyway.

There was a $100,000 bond to get out, but there was no way Johnson County was going to let that happen. The two original DUIs in Overland Park, they went ahead and dropped those, but Johnson County just sort of put them in their back pocket, just in case. If I found a way to get $10,000 to get bonded out, they would have just pulled those out again and thrown me back in jail. There was no way they were going to let me get back out on the streets.

After the arraignment, they evaluated me and I'm asking them why. They said they are trying to determine if I was going to be housed in a maximum-, medium- or minimum-class security pod at the regular jail on Gardner, Kansas. I couldn't believe that. I was thinking I was going to get out right away, but that's not how they talked to me, about where I was going to jail.

That whole time, I just tried to sleep a lot, because I was so depressed. I was stuck in jail and I knew it. Being held in that little cell with just a tiny window was like nothing I had ever experienced in my life. I slept nonstop trying not to think about what I had just done. I was basically left all alone and had no one to reach out to for help, no one to listen.

I was transferred to the jail in Gardner. I didn't know how long I was going to be there, but I knew I wasn't getting out anytime soon. I was in a horrible place. I did get minimum security – Pod 11-D, I'll never forget it – and when I walked in there were about 60 people and they all stopped what they were doing and watched me because they had been anticipating my arrival.

I remember the first time I tasted the food, I gagged and almost threw it up, it was so bad. I didn't eat for three days. I just remember returning the tray of food with everything on it and the vultures would rush at me to get the food I didn't eat. I couldn't believe it but they were all used to it. They would take whatever they could get.

I wasn't used to it at all, of course. The only good thing about getting to the jail in Gardner after five days was finally being able to get a hold of my parents.

***   ***   ***

The hardest part of being in jail is being stuck inside all the time. I was stuck in a pod, and you never see outside at all, 24 hours a day. It's extremely depressing. I slept in a 20-by-20 room with seven other guys. There were four bunk beds and it was really crowded. At Gardner, they turned off the lights at 11 and they didn't come back on till 6. Being under fluorescent lights all day changes you. My hair was different, my fingernails, my skin, everything, it just changed.

The worst is being stuck inside and never getting any fresh air. I felt like I was in a big closet 24/7 and it was horrible. You learned to sleep with the lights on and you learned to sleep through noise non-stop. I just tried to adapt to my surroundings.

Being something of a celebrity in jail isn't a good thing at all. The module officer told everybody in my pod that a big-time athlete was coming and they were all told that they were getting someone special in there. I don't know why they did it, because I hadn't played in a long time, but they still built it up. Everybody knew who I was before I got in there, but I really just kept to myself.

I hated the whole mindset of the whole system. It was like a revolving door. There were people inside when I got there and then a few months later, they would be back. And it was almost like a reunion. I just shook my head at all the repeat offenders who thought it was normal. They didn't think it was a big deal, but I say that all the time when I'm talking to kids that it is a big deal. I tell kids that jail is for losers. Normal people don't go to jail.

I sure didn't consider myself normal anymore. I was a loser, no doubt about it. That's how I felt, and it was depressing as hell to feel that way.

28

Chapter

GETTING SENTENCED TO TWO YEARS AND ADJUSTING TO JAIL

When I got transferred to Gardner, Kansas, they did it with me in handcuffs and shackles on a large bus, and that was incredibly humiliating. I got thrown into a pod with 60 other people and I tried to just stay to myself but that wasn't very easy.

All the inmates knew who I was, because the guards had told them I was coming, this big basketball star, which was a joke. They all just stopped and watched me come in and then they waited to see which cell I was going to be in. You shared these little 20-by-20 room with eight people, four bunks per room. As soon as you walk into your cell, you either talk or you don't. I didn't say a word. If someone wanted to introduce themselves to me, then I reciprocated but I did not go out of my way to make friends with anyone. I kept to myself.

Once I finally got a hold of my parents, I asked them to call Steve Sakoulas, who had been a friend of mine for years and was a great attorney in Kansas City. I met with him and he told me what I could expect. I expected to be there between 30 and 90 days, and was hoping for 30 at the most. I got settled in, figuring it was going to be a short stay.

But then on Dec. 20, I'm sitting in my cell and the guys are telling me that I am on TV. It turned out that my second ex-wife of six months, Nancy Dodik, started contacting every media outlet and told them all what was going on. The TV stations, newspapers, everything, they turned me into the big story of the day. Every time I went to court, they were all there. That was the worst, because I was handcuffed and shackled and I had to do the shackle-shuffle for the equivalent of about two football fields, going from the vehicle to the courtroom. And then all the cameras would be there, to record it all. I never expected that.

I'm thinking, after a few weeks, I'm going to be out and now I'm all over the media. Then my lawyer came to see me and he said "We've got a problem. Steve Howe, the Johnson County district attorney, is taking your case and he never does DUI cases. He's an elected official, so if he's taking your case, then he's going to want to make an example out of you."

My lawyer goes to Steve Howe and he said, "Two years." It was an election year and he's on TV all the time and he's always talking about me and how they are going to get tough on drunk driving. I was his poster boy for his entire campaign. My attorney Steve asked, "Why are you doing this to my client?" and Howe said, "One, because I can, and two because I want to make an example out of him."

And there was nothing we could do about it. It was a flat two years in jail and there was nothing we could do. Everyone else in a similar situation, they got 30 days or 90 days at the most. So I went from watching child molesters, burglars and other felons all come and go while I was still there. I watched one guy come and go who had 11 DUIs. Howe had me in his crosshairs and he really stuck it to me.

Sentencing day was traumatic for my kids because they came to court and spoke to the judge, but it didn't matter to the judge. That wacko Nancy Dodik came to court every time to try to make things worse on a constant basis. Every court hearing I had was packed with the media and the public as well as Nancy being nasty and also people from Mothers Against Drunk Driving.

I'm not complaining over being punished for what I did, but the system is what it is. They can do what they want and he was ready to make a big example out of me. Nothing my attorney told him made any kind of difference, in regard to what was going on in my life. My car accident, it didn't matter. I had character witnesses who wanted to help, with a job and with treatment, and every time he said no.

***   ***   ***

I blame all of the long sentence on my ex-wife Nancy. She was always filing suits against me for everything and she was always running to the media to make a big deal out of it. The judges would always tell her no when she tried to sue me for things, but she was always trying to mess with me to make sure the legal system put me down as much as it could.

Her family is wacko. Nancy constantly told me her father was a severe alcoholic and that he constantly beat on her mother. They were from Yugoslavia, and they were just crazy. Her father threatened to kill me several times. I actually slept with a 9mm gun at one point because I believed his death threats were real. He left me voicemail messages threatening me, but the police wouldn't arrest him because they said it wasn't a direct threat. I still have all those voicemail messages. He wanted to cut my arms and legs off and said that all the time in voicemails. They would stalk me at my house, park right out front, and try to threaten me. They would call my parents too, and leave horrible voicemail messages for them.

If it wasn't him, it was the mother or Nancy's sister. They were all horrible.

It got so bad that the Overland Park police finally arrested Nancy's sister Melanie and charged her for harassment. It was so bad that they put restraining orders against her, so she couldn't come near me or any of my children.

*** *** ***

Did I deserve some sort of punishment? Absolutely. But did I deserve something so excessive? I don't think so. I asked for mediation in front of a judge because I thought that I had been treated really unfairly by Steve Howe in the first place. It was five months later before it finally happened and the judge doing the mediation was Judge Kevin Moriarity.

I talked to the judge for a long time and he told me, "You sound like an educated guy and that things have gotten really bad in your life, but this is what you have to do. You have to put this behind you and get on with your life." He said "I am going to recommend you've done enough time in jail." He asked me if I was willing to go get treatment and I told him, 'Absolutely. I'll go. "

Judge Sara Welsh was my original sentencing judge. Judge Moriarity made that recommendation, but then Judge Welsh still said no. I waited five months for mediation and they had no interest in hearing his recommendation. They just said no, and didn't even consider it. So that was it. It was done.

We worked out the deal where I did one year in jail, then the therapeutic community and then the Oxford House, and all that. But we also agreed if I violated anything, I would have to go back to jail for two more years. I agreed with that, because I knew I wasn't going to do anything. But then when the time comes, they said three years instead of the two we agreed to. I said no, I'm not signing this agreement. And then right away, they're saying, "OK then, the deal is off and we're going after you for seven years in jail instead of two. We're going to give you the max on every charge." So I just signed it, and that was it. There was nothing I could do about it.

***   ***   ***

The worst thing about all of that was that I went to court several times and that was a most humiliating thing ever. Every time I would get handcuffed and shackled and it was hard. Being shackled, you couldn't even walk with your normal gait, so I just had to do the "shackle shuffle" in front of everybody. It was a media circus there every time. TV, newspapers, Mothers Against Drunk Driving, they were all there every time. I hadn't even played basketball for 15 years, and they made it look like I was some big-time basketball celebrity.

In Kansas City, I was nothing. No one all those years looked at me as an ex-player. I'm not even from Kansas City, and I was nothing to everyone there. But they sensationalized all of it. I was big news until there were some killings at the Jewish Community Center. Once that happened, they forgot about me. I didn't have to watch myself on TV with my fellow inmates after that.

***   ***   ***

Somebody told me once when I was in there that all I was

losing was time, that everything would be the same once I got out of jail, but as far as I was concerned, my whole life was getting taken away from me. You're told when to eat, when to sleep, when to shower, when to wake up, and you just do what you're told. I had a few friends who put money on my books every once a while, because if you don't you'll starve in there.

I basically went on a vegan diet while I was in there, and I did that mostly for the peanut butter. For breakfast I would have fruit and one scoop of peanut butter and two tortillas and that was it. That was my best meal of the day. I would hide the peanut butter and tortillas in a cup and that would be my snack back in my room later in the day. For lunch and dinner I just got beans and rice and a vegetable and that was it. I lost 55 pounds doing that, just starving. Commissary day is like Christmas in there, guys getting $60 in snacks every week. I never got to do that. I didn't have any money. Toward the end I got a little bit, but that was it. People would freak out if the commissary lady didn't show up on time.

The commissary stuff was things you'd bet with too. I'd run football pools and people would bet desserts. People would play cards for snacks, pinochle or spades. It was so depressing, and to be there for a full year seemed like forever. I literally spent most of my day reading books, more than 100 during my time there, and writing in my journal.

People would make alcohol in jail from juice packets, oranges and some honey buns or something of that sort for their sugar and yeast to ferment things. The hardest thing for those guys was hiding that stuff, because they shook down our rooms all the time looking for contraband. There were drugs in jail too, but I had no interest. I really didn't. There wasn't a time where I ever felt like "Man, I've got to have this." I never felt that way in jail. I stayed away from it and it never bothered me at all.

I never had any problems with any of the other inmates. I pretty much kept to myself and let it be. It's a county jail, and inmates were coming and going all the time. I got to be a 'pod-father" after a while because I was one of the elders. So all that meant was I had control over the TV and no one could change it unless I said so. I also got the "privilege" of cleaning the pod at night after everyone was locked down in their cells. The guards would ask me if I wanted to watch a football game and they would turn it on for me while I was cleaning. Oh, the little things.

The whole legal thing was a total nightmare. It's still so surreal to me. I still can't believe I went to jail, because I always followed all the rules in my life. But, I guess I deserved it. I started pushing the boundaries for a long time, then I finally started pushing beyond the boundaries. I didn't care anymore. I had no self-esteem anymore and I didn't care. And I paid for it. It was a humiliating experience. There were a lot of crazy people in there and they all had a lot of crazy stories. I saw some guys circle through three or four times. They all had crazy stories, and to know that you're there, you're one of them. It was very humbling and humiliating.

I had one or two friends who came to visit, but that was it and it wasn't very often. I didn't really like having visitors because it was just so hard after they left.

Spending two years probably was enough to change me. If it had only been 30 days, I probably wouldn't have changed. I would have gone right back to the way I was living before then. And it wasn't like I had any sort of 'A, ha" moment or anything, it just came over time that I just didn't ever want to be in this situation again, this situation of sitting in jail day after day, feeling horrible about myself.

One thing you get used to is being able to actually stay pretty serene in jail. There was a sense of peace and calm, because

195

I didn't have court dates or people hassling me or lots of things pulling at me.

At least all of that was over.

29

Chapter

VISITS WITH MY
PARENTS AND KIDS IN JAIL

Once **I was settled** in at Gardner and I knew I wasn't
going anywhere for a year, I just tried to get into a routine that
would help the days pass as fast as they could. I didn't talk to many
people inside, by choice, so I read a lot and I started keeping a
journal that I wrote in every day.

I had a couple of friends who would come see me every
once in a while, but it wasn't very often. To be honest, I didn't really have many friends at the time and the guys I spent the most time
with, my party friends, they weren't about to come visit me in jail.

My parents? They came twice. I had to beg and beg for
them to come the first time. And the second time? It only lasted a
few minutes and I walked away.

And I haven't seen them since.

It's all with good reason, too. What they did to me was so
off the charts that I have never heard of other parents ever hurting
their own child so badly. After my arrest, once it become obvious
that I wasn't going to be able to get right out, I called and called
them, and it was days before they came to see me. When they were
there, I talked to them about some things that I needed to take care
of. I needed a lawyer, I needed my house and cars watched and I

needed some bills paid. I asked them to take care of that stuff for me.

I was also very concerned about my kids and I asked them to help there, too. None of it got done. So when they came to visit the second time, I asked them if they had done those things. One answer after another was no, no, no. They weren't going to help, so I got up and walked away. I knew what they were doing.

And what they were doing was trying to destroy everything I had worked for in my life and take everything else I had. They deceived me to the very end. They literally sold, threw away or took everything I owned.

How did they do it? Sort of like that district attorney who had it in for me, they did it because they could. And they did it because they knew there was nothing I could do about it. They had all the cards because almost 20 years ago, when I was playing professional basketball overseas, I gave them a power of attorney to handle a few things for me here in the U.S. While I was in France or Switzerland or Argentina, I would need them to do things here. I would send them money and I would have them move things around for me, investment-wise, and I would have them pay for certain things. It worked fine, and then once I moved back, it wasn't an issue any more. I did everything myself.

But they still had that power of attorney. And boy, did they use it. They sold my house without my knowledge, and sold it for hundreds of thousands of dollars less than it was worth. And the proceeds from the sale? They kept it all. They told me in a letter that their retirement accounts were not doing well.

They just lied to my face both times they came to see me. Now I know why. Their whole intent was to deceive me and steal everything I had left in my life. They promised me in jail that my home would be fine and they would take care of things, but after three months in jail I get a letter from them telling me they had used the power of attorney to sell my house. They gave away my house more than they sold it. It was a half-million dollar house and it hardly had any mortgage left on it. It sold in one day – of course – because they had set the asking price so low.

At that point in my life, the equity that I had in the house was basically all the money I had left in life. Not only did they steal my home and keep the money, but they got rid of all the furniture, too. Even all my clothes, they just got rid of it all. They threw most of it away and said it was junk, which was ridiculous. Everything that was special to me was gone. I had hundreds of pieces of memorabilia from all my stops in life, sports memorabilia as well as beautiful art work from all over the world. To this day I have only gotten a few pieces back. They still have the rest of it.

I was furious when I got the news in a letter and just wanted to die. It really was the first I had heard of it. Even my attorney who was taking care of my legal issues had no idea what they were doing. The answer they gave me in their letter was that their retirement was not doing so well.

They even cost me my car. It was a $130,000 BMW and there were only a few payments left. It was probably still worth $50,000 or $60,000 at least, but they just gave it back to the banks without my knowledge. It easily could have been sold if I had known about it. I also had a beautiful 500 SL Mercedes that I still haven't gotten back. So everything that was precious to me in life has been taken and stripped away. What they did to my house and all my belongings had me in one of the darkest places in life I had ever been in. I went days and days in jail, just shaking. I hated what they had done.

But I guess I really shouldn't be surprised. When I played college basketball, they only came to a few of my games. And all those years as a pro? They never saw me play once, hundreds and hundreds of games, and they never saw one. And there were plenty of times I offered to fly them somewhere to come see me. They always said no. My father didn't even come to my wedding, that's how little he cared about me.

Three years have passed since then and I still don't talk to them. My mother reaches out now and then, through my kids, or through my girlfriend Jamie, but that's it. I've gotten some of my memorabilia back, but not much. And the money? Well, that's another story.

***   ***   ***

I've said more than a few times already that you should never want to be in jail. It's a place for losers. You have no privacy, you have no rights and you definitely aren't getting rehabilitated one bit. The food was horrible, but what was the absolute worst was the medical care if you did get sick.

One time in Gardner I got transferred to medical segregation because I was getting extremely sick from an abscess under a crown on my tooth. I was in incredible pain. But they refused to fix it and only wanted to pull it. I said "You're not pulling any tooth, especially one that just got crowned a little while ago.

So it became a standoff. I refused to have it pulled and they refused to fix it. They're like, that's what we do here. "I'm like, I just paid for that crown. You're not ripping it all out of my mouth." I ended up getting really sick and it lasted for like a month. They gave me a few antibiotics, but that didn't help. Finally they were forced to take me to get a root canal, which is what should have been done in the first place. They were really mad at me for all of that, so once I left med segregation, they transferred

200

me to a different pod so I had to get to know everyone new again.

They treat you like crap in there, and I guess rightfully so, But still, you've got to have some human rights in there. That was a year of hell. I'm glad I didn't have anything else wrong with me. I probably would have died in there.

*** *** ***

I was able to keep in touch with my four oldest daughters pretty well, thanks to my ex-wife Lara. She was really good about bringing them by for visits. It was hard at Gardner though, because there was no personal contact. I would be on a TV monitor and so were they, and we could just talk. It was very hard on them. She would bring one different daughter each week to see me.

It was very hard on me, too. I loved seeing them, of course, but it broke my heart as well. Every time they'd come for a visit, I'd go back in my cell and really had to work hard to fight off the tears.

My relationship with my ex-wife was actually pretty good at the time. She came every week. She brought the kids and even brought my clothes when I got out of there. It was good, and friendly, although that would change later when the money situation changed. Then it got very ugly, legally. But I give her this: She always tried to make it easier on the kids. It was hard to see me there in those clothes and to be confined, but they got used to it, at least as much as you can get used to it.

A child should never have to see their father in jail or put them through the pain and suffering that I did by creating this humiliating experience for them. They did not deserve to go through this, and it still hurts me to this day to know what I put them through. It was hard for all of us to keep our emotions in check.

201

They all cried like crazy the first time they came to visit.

So did their Dad.

I missed a few things that year that really hurt. My daughter Adriana, she was playing basketball her senior year, and all the parents walked everyone out at the last home game and I couldn't be there because I was in jail. That was embarrassing and very hurtful for her, because everyone in that gym knew where I was. I knew I was missing it that night, and I sat in my cell, just torn up.

There's nothing I hate worse than hurting my kids.

30

Chapter

FROM JAIL TO A THERAPEUTIC COMMUNITY, WITH LOTS OF CHANGE

I was so relieved to get out of the county jail in Gardner and go to the next step in my sentence, which was a therapeutic community that was supposed to help me with my so-called drug and alcohol issues.

Walking out of jail was one of the happiest days of my life. I wasn't outside for a year. The only time I ever saw the sun that first year was when I had to leave to go to court for something or go to the doctor or dentist. When you spend a year locked inside under those fluorescent lights with no sunshine, it changes you. My skin turned a pale white color, like there was no pigment left, my fingernails turned weird and you could tell just being inside that my complexion had completely changed. So going to the therapeutic community was a great change.

You were still incarcerated at the TC, but it was like night and day. It felt like heaven just to get to listen to the radio or have regular TV channels to watch when time allowed. It was more like a dorm than jail. You wore normal clothes and you could go outside all the time. It was still corrections, and I couldn't leave, but it was so different. Just walking outside was so nice. Even working in the kitchen all weekend was nice, just to get out of the facility

203

IN THEIR OWN WORDS

**Mike Tompkins, Recovery Director
& Co-Owner of Tompkins Industries**

I didn't think much of Todd Jadlow the first time I met him in person. In fact, he made me so mad that I started yelling at him about five minutes after I met him.

I went to speak to a group of about 40 inmates who were incarcerated because of some legal issue related to drugs or alcohol. All I did was ask them if they were all dealing with some addiction problem. Everyone raised their hand but Todd, who was sitting in the back of the room with that non-caring look on his face, like I was wasting his time.

The dude had been in jail for more than a year already, and he didn't think he had a problem?

I let in to him right on the spot. Who gets two DUIs in one day? Who drives 121 miles an hour down the highway drunk with a 2-year-old in the car? What makes you think you're something special?

I knew who he was, so I got after him hard. I didn't care that he was a basketball player and I told him I'd match paychecks with him any time. It really ticked me off that he didn't think he had a problem.

It's guys like him who always get under my skin. Look, he had four DUIs in six months, so it was obvious to me that nothing was going to deter him from acting like an idiot.

I walked out of that therapeutic community and I was still angry. I hated his holier than thou attitude.

A few days later, I got a call from Todd that he wanted to talk to me. I have to tell you, I was shocked by that. I didn't think he cared at all.

I was glad I was wrong.

and do something different. We didn't have jobs at the TC, but I always volunteered to work in the kitchen, and I loved it.

We had meetings all the time, and these councils where you disciplined people if you had to. It was a joke. The counselors didn't care about anybody, they were just making sure you were passing time. Mine was a joke. She would proctor the group sessions and that was it. She was pregnant so she was checked out. It was a complete waste of time and you got nothing out of it.

Not that I necessarily cared to get anything out of it. I spent a year in jail and never once considered myself an alcoholic or a drug addict, and this always caused a problem with the counselors and everyone else because I refused to call myself either. I choose to think that my life got completely out of control and I made horrible decisions that led to the self-destruction of my life. Another part that played a huge impact on my life was the severe depression I was in. I truly lost my will to live and just wanted to die. I did not care anymore whether I lived or died, and am extremely thankful and lucky that I did not physically hurt anyone else along the way. To me the words alcoholic and drug addict are very demeaning and vulgar, and I refuse to place an adjective on myself such as referring to myself as either of those. I am a person in recovery, recovery from a whole lot of bad stuff.

I looked at going to jail this way, that my time had run out and it was time to pay the piper for pressing the boundaries for so long and getting away with it. In essence, my time had run out and luck was no longer on my side.

Everyone had issues though, and since there were no drugs or alcohol around, of course, people had massive cravings for tobacco, which wasn't allowed either. I don't use any kind of tobacco but that was a big thing in there. People would use smokeless tobacco all the time and there was a big black market for it inside.

People out on visits would stick chews of smokeless tobacco in a glove up their butt to sneak it in, and then they would sell them for a dollar a chew. It was crazy. I couldn't imagine that.

There were about 40 people in there but it was more like a cult. Every minute of your day was scheduled and there was no getting around it. You did group meetings with a counselor four times a week. From 8 in the morning until 11, you met for an hour with your counselor, then you did book work for two hours. I did all mine in a few weeks, and for five months I didn't have anything to do. But you couldn't lay in your bed during that time. It was strict as to where you could be, and there was a lot of time just doing absolutely nothing.

To be honest, it was probably worse than jail, for how your days went, because I had no interest in talking about addiction or what my alcohol use meant to me. I wasn't interested in getting help for any of that, because I never considered that I had any kind of abuse. The only thing better than jail was being able to be outside and to go places, but the program itself was a joke.

And then a guy named Mike Tompkins showed up one day, and my life changed.

Just like that, it changed forever.

*** *** ***

Mike Tompkins came to the therapeutic center about three months into my visit. He ran an Oxford House, which was basically a halfway house for some people who were alcoholics and addicts who were transitioning from the legal system back into the real world. Mike had his own abuse past, but did a lot of great work now talking to people about drug and alcohol issues.

When he showed up that day, of course I had no interest in listening to him. He was speaking to the whole group, all 40 of us, and I was just sitting in the back, not listening and minding my own business. Mike asked the group – and a group, mind you, that all had been arrested on some form or drug or alcohol issue – who thought they had some sort of drug or alcohol problem.

Thirty-nine hands went up. Mine didn't. I just sat in the back, head down.

So Mike started railing on me from the podium. "I know who you are," he yells. "I know what you did, I know all the things you did. And you think you can sit here like you're something special, like you're better than everybody? Let me tell you this, you're a worthless piece of crap. You don't think you have a problem? Then you're a dumb ass too." He just went on an on at me for several minutes, and he didn't let up. He was angry and he was taking it out on me, calling me a big shot about every other sentence.

Normally I would just laugh that kind of stuff off, but he struck a nerve with me. I had a year in jail behind me, and three months in TC, although I wasn't really buying into their mind games. To this day I don't know why, but I went to one of the counselors a few days later and asked to get Mike's number, so we could talk. That's not like me to do that. If I didn't know you, I didn't want to know you. But for some reason, I felt compelled to talk to Mike.

We started talking and that's how we started to get to know each other. We talked once or twice a month for the last three months I was there in the TC. He's really hard core when it comes to recovery, and he wanted me to open up my head and my heart a little bit and learn to accept what was wrong with me.. He likes to call people addicts and junkies and all that and I don't go there. It's the Narcotics Anonymous way for him, and I don't like to call myself that. But Mike is great. He's real hard core about recovery and he's been right there for me since then. For everything that's gotten better in my life, I owe a lot of that to Mike.

Before starting to talk to Mike, I was still just incredibly angry about everything. Jail is a breeding ground for nothing more than increasing your criminal behavior once you get out. It doesn't change you. Jail didn't do that.

You go into jail knowing one drug dealer and you come out knowing 20. That's why I say all the time that people who say going to jail is no big deal are so wrong. It is a big deal. Jail is for losers. Even if it's only 30 days or six months, it is a big deal. Normal people don't go to jail.

Mike has been that big of an impact for me, because he showed me another way. He's showed me how to get back to lead-

Me and my girls the year before I went to jail.

ing a normal life again, and that's huge for me. Before I met Mike at TC, I never thought normal was ever going to be an option for me.

***   ***   ***

Volunteering to work in the kitchen was fun for me, because it gave me something to do, and I even took other guy's shifts on the weekends, just so I could be down there and out of my room. I worked Friday, Saturday and Sunday and it was nice to actually eat fresh hot food. It was the same bad food as jail but at least it was hot and fresh. We'd go down there and sneak hamburgers when we could.

At TC you were allowed to go out for doctor's appointments and such, but every time you went out, they would drug test you and test for alcohol when you came back, and they would strip-search you too, right on down to spreading your butt checks. That was so humiliating. And if you did something, they'd send you back to jail. That happened to a lot of guys I was in there with, they would violate and get sent back to jail and start over. I never tested it, of course, and I passed every test every time I went out.

While I was in TC, I was allowed to go out on passes to see my youngest daughter, Camryn. Because of what I had done, I had lost my custodial rights to her, but was allowed to see her under a monitored and supervised setting. After working over a month to get her mother Nancy to comply with the court orders for my daughter to see me, I was able to start the reintegration with her at TFI in Lawrence. She did everything she could to try to block me and keep me from seeing my daughter. If it was left up to her, she would have never let me see my daughter again. Yes, she is that type of mother. She did not want my daughter to see me or for me to have any type of relationship with her. That's just the way she was and the way she will always be.

She would always try to mess with me. Nancy would call the district attorney nonstop, trying to cause trouble for me by making up every lie that she could to try to derail me from getting out.

Once I was allowed to go out to see my youngest daughter for supervised visits, my other four daughters would often come to pick me up, so I could see all of them on the same day. The TC people gave me some extra time, so my daughters would go eat lunch with me, either on the way there or on the way back.

My youngest daughter's mom, that witch Nancy, found out about that and she would call the judge and the district attorney and she would do anything she could to get me in trouble. She would call the DA and ask why he was running around, because she wanted me to go back to jail. She would lie to them, telling me I was drinking and running around Lawrence, which was a huge lie. All we did was grab food on my way to the appointment or on the way back. It was maybe 15 or 20 minutes max and it was always right on the way back and forth. I went into their house once for two minutes to see my dog, but that was only for a few minutes and it was right there at their house. Those were monumental days, being out and seeing my daughters.

I talked with the counselors when I was getting ready to leave the TC and they told me that there's a 97 percent recidivism rate – or failure rate – for those who go through programs and probations like this in Johnson County. They only hope to plant a seed. But everyone is ordered to go there, so a lot of people don't care if they succeed or not. I have to admit I was in that non-caring group when I got there, but then Mike Tompkins helped me open my mind and get me to listen to things being said. In my mind, I was already going to do whatever it took to never come back to this place again. It was definitely a checkmark off my bucket list.

Maybe I'll be part of that three percent that makes it.

After TC, I had three months in a transition center where you could be out all day if you had a job to go to. I went to work for my girlfriend Jamie at her company, Social Suppers. You had freedom to come and go, and it was nice to get a little work done. It was nice because it allowed me to get a routine back. I prepared high-end gourmet meals for people to take home and cook. The meals were prepared with the freshest of ingredients and sent home for the people to simply cook. You could say Social Suppers is like Blue Apron on steroids. All you have to do is follow the instructions to cook the food; it is already prepared for you. That's what I did. I helped prepare the gourmet meals as well as tend to customers who came in. I just basically gave great customer service.

It worked great for me to be out doing something. It was more of an opportunity for freedom, and it was a step in the right direction.

31

Chapter

THE FINAL STEP
FROM HOME, OXFORD HOUSE

Once **I graduated** from the TC and finished my three months working from the residential center, the last step to being released was staying three months at the Oxford House, which is something of a halfway house. I really liked it there, and not only because it was the last step to getting back to being on the outside again. It was also a nice reminder of my first steps on this horrible journey, because it looked directly at the back side of the jail in Olathe where I spent my first five days incarcerated. It was a great constant reminder for me to where I had been and where I was now.

It was helpful for me because Mike Tompkins also lived there at Oxford House. He was instrumental in getting me there and we did a lot of work there on my recovery. It was a great step for me in getting my life heading in the right direction. I would go to probation meetings from there, and go to my court-ordered counseling. I started to attend a lot of NA meetings with Mike and I really got involved with him in doing the step work that's really a key component of any 12-step program.

Oxford House is a perfect set-up, because it's like a democracy and you can do what you want, so I could see my kids

213

quite a bit. I liken it to a fraternity. There are eight guys in the house, but you hardly see anybody because everyone's always out working or doing their thing. You paid $100 a week to live there and that was for everything, and that was even for food. Hi-Vee donated food to the house, and we actually ate pretty well there. For the first time in almost two years, I kind of got my appetite back, and I started to eat healthy on a regular basis again.

There was still drug and alcohol testing there because it was still part of your jail sentence being there, and if you failed, you had 30 minutes to pack up and leave. Those were the rules, and I saw it happen a time or two. It was never a problem for me, but a few people didn't make it.

Mike really pushed me through with the authorities to get a spot for me at Oxford House. They had to take a vote to get me in, but he made sure it got done. He's been a life saver. He said he believes in me. I spent three months there and it was a huge help for me. Mike stayed at Oxford House himself after what he went through and he really puts a lot of time and effort into it. He's been there in Olathe at Oxford House for five years and he's loved it.

Mike is rough when it comes to staying clean and working a program of recovery, but he's got a great heart. He's a really good guy. He's made some dreams come true for me already. Being at Oxford House was a great experience for me. I think it really set the stage for getting back to normal in the real world again.

Those three months, I got to spend a lot of time with my girls, and I spent time with my girlfriend Jamie and we had a lot of long talks when I was working. I went to a ton of meetings, too, and that was a big help.

The best thing to come out of Oxford House, though, were all the long, long talks I would have with Mike. We would spend hours and hours talking about what I wanted to do with my future, and I how I wanted to go about living my life the right way. I was ready for my two-year nightmare with the legal system to be over.

That last day, I packed all my stuff and gave Mike a big hug. And then I walked out the door, stuck in the legal system for the very last time.

I closed the door and walked out. It was time to go home … and start my life all over again.

32

Chapter

GOING HOME, AND
STARTING OVER WITH MY KIDS

Once it was time to actually come home, I decided to move from Overland Park to Lawrence to be closer to my girls. I leased a house in Lawrence and my ex-wife and I agreed to share custody of the two youngest girls, where they would live with me half the time and with her half the time.

I had the same responsibilities as every normal parent, right from the first day, picking them up from school, doing their sporting events, getting their food, everything. Honestly, it wasn't that big of a change for me, because we shared custody before and I was ready for my life to be that way again after two years of being away. I really wanted that. But the biggest challenge coming home after two years was trying to deal with a 16-year-old who had been given a green light to do anything and everything she wanted to in life with no repercussions or no consequences for her actions.

I've always been about discipline and following rules as a parent, but my ex-wife Lara and I often didn't see eye-to-eye on that. My 16-year-old, Sofia, wasn't following any rules or boundaries and I had to change that, and, of course, that was a difficult adjustment for both of us. I was just so happy to be out again, and to be able to see my kids and do every day normal things. Part of

217

that too, though, was being a Dad, and trying to do what I could to help her live her life the right way.

I was just trying to give her some balance to where she could understand it. I tried to get her to understand that there are rules and I tried to give her the reasons why they are so important. When I was gone, she wasn't going to school and when she was there, she wasn't doing very well. She'd stay out all night and not care about any kind of curfews, and I knew that had to change. There's a reason why there are rules in place and if you don't follow the rules, you have to face the consequences. She had just basically been running wild the past couple of years she didn't live with me. I had to reel her in a bit, and the more time we got to spend together, the better it got over time. My younger one, Kiara, lived with me too, and she's never been an issue. She's very respectful and she's one of those kids who just sort of follows the rules and does the right thing. It was great to be around her again. So it was really great just picking up where I left off.

Without all the drinking and drugs, of course.

The hardest part of parenting for me was seeing them so set in their ways and the way they did things was so different from what I am used to. I have always been regimented. If I've got a time to be somewhere, I'm going to be there on time. Being on time, that's some of that life stuff that Coach Knight taught me.

My two oldest daughters, Alexia and Adriana, were off to school, but I still got to see them quite a bit, too. The other two have lived with me in the past, as well. My second oldest, she lived with me her junior year in high school, but she got in a little trouble and couldn't go to prom. So she decided to go back and live with her mom. Disciplining them and showing them a different way has been hard. They go back with their mom, and that never works, so they leave again. The hardest thing to understand is why they don't see what I've lost and why it's not a deterrent factor more for them. They get in trouble more than once, and I don't see how they can do that.

When I'm out speaking to groups about all that I've been through, the hardest questions I have to answer are usually about my kids. That's still hard on me. Sometimes I've gotten to a point where I can emotionally check out, but it's hard. Anything about my kids is still hard. I've asked them to come with me to a talk sometime, but we haven't gotten there yet. I think that will be pretty powerful, when the time comes. They aren't really there, though. They know I go around speaking, but they don't want to be involved and they don't even really ask me much about it. If I didn't say something, they wouldn't know anything about what I've done. I know there's still some pain there. They only thing they ever mention is "Please don't speak in Lawrence." Or "Please don't speak at my school." I think that would embarrass them too much.

We're working on it all. I think, like anyone, it will take time. My kids, unless I bring it up, will never bring anything up to me. They are older now and into their routines, and we disagree a lot of times on what they should be doing. I'm trying to not be too overbearing, and I try to think about it from their perspective. But when they get in a little trouble, I can't just say "That's OK." I try to explain it to them, that they can't act that way. I discipline them because I care. It's just night and day between my house and their mom's house. We all have to adjust.

They've never really talked much about my time in jail, or what I was doing to get there. Sometimes they would ask questions when we were in the car, because I always have to blow into the Inter-Lock devise to start my car. A few times they ask, "Why do you have to do that?" or "How long do you have to do that?" That

Inter-Lock devise has to be in my car until 2019 and it's a constant reminder of the past, present and the future to me. The girls and I, we're getting there. We've had a lot of fun days together, all of us. It's nice to have them back.

*** *** ***

The biggest battles I still have are with my second wife Nancy over the time I get to spend with my youngest child Camryn now that I'm out. She has made it so difficult on me from the very beginning. She dragged me in and out of court for years, even when I was in jail. And it's not really about the time I spend with my daughter with her, it always just comes back to money. She always figures if she has my daughter more, that she should get more money. It's always about money, because she was a gold-digger from the start.

Everybody warned me about her, but I did not listen and I will be paying for those consequences for many years to come. Getting involved with her has been by far the biggest mistake of my life, far worse than spending time in jail. I have been in and out of court cases with her since the time I met her in September of 2009. The only thing that has been accomplished with all this is making me poor and making the lawyers rich.

It's been a true nightmare. That's what you get when you meet someone and three months later you're convinced to marry this person. Whatever came over me, I don't know, it was definitely a lack of sanity and another poor decision on my part. It was clear I was under the influence of heavy chemicals when I met her and later it was found out that she was too, because Nancy tested positive for cocaine on two different occasions in court-ordered drug screens and lost custody of her older kids. So it was clear I was not the only one under the influence.

The one great thing that did come out of meeting her was Camryn, whom I love and care about more than anything. But that was the only good thing.

***   ***   ***

Because Camryn was in the car with me when I got arrested, the spotlight was on me about being a bad dad with her, but I tell everyone that I have always loved that girl to death and I always will. I love our time together and have from the beginning. So putting that all back together has been hard.

My visits with her after I went to jail all had to be supervised and it was really hard. The first time we met after those two years, we had to do it in a family-care facility so it could be monitored. She was only four years old, and she hadn't seen me in 16 months, and the first time she came into the room, she wouldn't even talk to me. She kept saying "No. No, Daddy." Her mother and her family were always telling her negative things. All she did was turn her head to get a glimpse of me, but her eyes told me the whole story, that I had hurt her. If her eyes could speak, you could tell they were saying "Why did you leave me? Where did you go? Why did you abandon me?" I really hurt her because I just disappeared. It was like 15 seconds, the first visit. That was is.

After several longer visits at the family services center and through a progression of parenting time, I wound up getting home visits every other weekend with Camryn, from 6 p.m. Friday to 6 p.m. Sunday. Every Wednesday I have her for two hours. The final court ruling on custody and child support and the parenting plan is coming up on Oct. 26 and I'm very anxious about that. I've been waiting for that day for a long time.

*** *** ***

My relationship with my parents is still non-existent, and that's fine. The stuff that went on while I was in jail, with them taking my house and keeping most of my money and belongings, I just can't get over that. I've gotten a few things back, but to do the things they did without any remorse or thoughts whatsoever, I can't get over it and I have no desire to have them in my life.

To me, they're dead to me. I still have a hard time coming to grips with what they did to my house. I don't understand it, to take the most prized possession that I had, to sell it and then tell me in a letter what they did after promising to take care of my house for me. My mother has reached out a few times to talk, but I've resisted. That was all I had left, and they took almost all of it.

I have no desire to fix anything with them. I'm just done with them. It's a difficult situation, and I choose not to think about it. It's a dead subject as far as I'm concerned. It just makes me mad, still. To this day, I still drive by my house once a week or so and I think about what they did to me. That was my house, and I loved it so much.

*** *** ***

Being home was great and all, but my life was by no means normal. I was still dealing with a lot of issues with the courts, mostly over child support and custody issues. I had some tax issues too, but I have been able to resolve all of those and that's made me feel good. Every day was still stressful because I felt like I was starting all over.

Living in Lawrence, I basically kept to myself. All the friends I had when I was drinking, they're all gone now, and that's fine. I have no interest in going back to that life, and I can't really be friends with those people, because they're still out there partying and I can't do that.

I definitely dealt with depression a lot because it was hard to start from scratch and put my life back together little by little. Having the kids was great, and working a little bit was great too, although it was often frustrating that I couldn't do more. Having the felonies, I couldn't get back in the medical field like I was and that's too bad.

Going forward, I have other plans. And I'm excited about it. It's 2016 now, and I'm heading in a new direction. I have been involved with mentoring others with addiction issues through the Welcome House in Kansas City and I have volunteered and done speaking engagements for another recovery program called First Call of Kansas City. I have really enjoyed speaking to high school and college students and it's nice to be moving forward.

One step at a time.

33

Chapter

STARTING THE TODD JADLOW
"GIVE IT BACK FOUNDATION"

Once I met Mike Tompkins and we started having in-depth conversations about all that I had been through, one thing always came out of it. He wanted to know what my life was going to be like once I got out of jail and if I had the strength and motivation to do things right.

I know I want to do things right. Heck, to be honest, I've always felt that way and that's how I have lived almost all of my life. I had a rough stretch there, though, and that says a lot about me, I think. What it tells me is that bad things can happen to anybody, even someone like me who has been considered to be a successful person for most of my life.

What I have come to know and understand is that no matter how bad things get and how far down that path you go in the wrong direction, there is always a way to come back and always a way to recover. Just look at me. I am a perfect example of this. It truly is not about drugs and alcohol, but about self-esteem and having the ability to love yourself enough to not put these chemicals into our body to change us, to make us someone we're not.

I want to make that clear. Drugs and alcohol were never the problem, I was the problem, I had to fix me. Drugs and alcohol

225

were the solution to my problem at the time, and a bad solution at that.

And that's my point, that bad things can happen, even to good people. So the more we talked about it, the more it made sense to me that if I went out in public and told my story, that maybe I could help people not go through all that pain and humiliation that I went through.

We talked about the best ways of doing that, and that's when the idea of the Todd Jadlow Give It Back Foundation came to be. The name says it all, really. I want to give back to the community and help anyone who needs help dealing with drug or alcohol issues, or needs help with finding a sober living environment. I want to help young people especially, because they are still impressionable, Drugs and alcohol can be a powerful thing that can overwhelm them if they don't have the tools to deal with it right.

Mike was instrumental in helping me get the foundation set up, along with a handful of other people. My girlfriend Jamie was a huge help too, because she worked tirelessly talking to schools and getting speaking engagements set up at schools. Without all her work, it may have never happened. At the beginning, she was just as important as Mike was to getting the foundation off the ground.

Just as importantly, talking about my struggles and my recovery helps me, too, because every time I am out speaking at a foundation event, it's a hard-hitting reminder of what I have put myself through, and what I've put my children and loved ones through. It's also a great reminder of how much better I feel now by staying clean and living life the right way. That's why the mission statement of our foundation is so simple. Our primary goal is to reach one child, one person or one family and make a difference in their lives.

When I was in the therapeutic community, in our group settings I told people when I got out that I wanted to do some public speaking and tell my story. I remember one guy laughing at me. He was asking me, "Why would anyone listen to you?" I get it. Because at the time, I was just an incarcerated criminal like he was. But the whole idea of speaking and telling my story started there. I don't know why. But I knew if I did it, I would have to be honest and be true. If I'm going to walk the walk and talk the talk, I'm going to be honest all the time.

My speaking keeps me on that path of not deviating. There's no way I could speak if I was doing anything with drugs and alcohol. There's no way to cover that up, so it's a good way to keep me focused on what I'm doing. When I went to Oxford House, I had no intent of going to meetings. I really wasn't interested. Mike Tompkins, he pushed me to go, and when I did, it wasn't as bad as I thought it was going to be. All the talking wasn't about drugs and alcohol, it was more about living your life a certain way, and dealing with issues. That was a step in the right direction for me, too, to accept what was wrong with me and being willing to do something about it.

I had been going to church again, so when they started talking about spiritual principles in NA, it hit home with me and I enjoyed it and could relate to it. One time after the meeting, a group of us went out and there were a lot of people who were really successful people. They owned car dealerships and real estate offices, and when I saw them, it really inspired me quite a bit because it was a great reminder that even the most successful people in the world still have to deal with issues like this. Being a part of that smaller group made you feel more accountable, too, because I didn't want to be letting anybody down.

When I was in Oxford House, as part of my probation

through Johnson County, they gave me a Life Coach, too. Her name was Jill Dollins and she would look at my talk when I was writing it, and she would look it over as I added to it. She helped me become a counselor for The Welcome House and I do that every week. Then she got me with a group called The First Call, and I met with the director of that group. I'm an ambassador with them too. That's been good for me, and I've been helping people too, which is good. They have partnered up with the foundation, and that's a good thing.

There's no hiding when I'm so involved. It gives me direction, gives me a purpose again. Every time I give a talk, it's like getting ready for a basketball game. It's empowering to give a talk and give my time. I'm a true believer in karma, and I think for whatever I give out, I'll get it back ten-fold.

I'm becoming a better person too through all this. With women, I was horrible, and I would just go through one after another. Now I'm trying to change all that. By speaking, it allows me to start down that path to be a better person in every area of my life.

*** *** ***

Part of my probation condition that has meant a lot to me is being able to spend time with Jill Dollins. I would meet with her every week, and it was always time well spent. She has put me in touch with the director of the Welcome House, Jamie Boyle, whom I met with and was offered a volunteer position of a lay counselor for the House. She also introduced me to Michelle Irwin, the director of First Call of Kansas City. They have partnered up with my Foundation and we do speaking events together at various schools and colleges in and around the Kansas City metro area.

After saying a prayer to God in TC and asking him to show me a better way to live or take me the hell out of here, I started a journal in which I wrote letters to God every day, which it was rightfully titled "Letters to God." I simply wrote a letter to God every day as well as doing daily prayers in both the morning and evening. In TC, I started my way back to Christ and asked him for forgiveness and asked him to please lead me down that right path and to serve him with purpose.

Ever since that day, my relationship with Christ has gotten stronger and stronger, and all the good things that have happened to me in my life I can attribute to God through his love and kindness. He truly is my inspiration and is leading the way for me in my recovery and comeback in life. Through Christ all good things happen and it is for me.

*** *** ***

Doing all this the right way has helped me open up my heart and my head. I'm going to church again now since I've been released and I feel a lot better about doing that too. I grew up in a staunch Catholic family, from my grandmother on down, and I was always used to going to church every day, being in Catholic schools.

Religion and God has always been a factor in my life, but when I quit playing basketball, I got away from everything. I got away from my spirituality and seeking help about being a better person. That was my way for many, many years. Until I was in the TC, I just finally said a prayer, saying "God, either show me a better way to live, or take me out of here."

229

I go to church all the time. And little things now, like being an usher, that matters to me about being involved in the community. Most of the time, I go to St. Michael's in Leawood, Kansas and I really get a lot out it, and I enjoy being a part of that parish and that community. It is my home when I am there.

Recently I went to confession for the first time in years. I hadn't been to confession is 32 years and the priest perked up when I told him that. He said he felt honored that I had picked him to listen to me. I told him I had committed every sin in the book, too many to list one at a time and I needed forgiveness for all of them. That was really important to me. It was the first time since high school that I had done it. He said a prayer, gave me a penance to do, and he absolved me of my sins. It made me feel better, just having that clean slate. I have never felt so free as I did that day after serving my penance and leaving church. Having that presence in my life at church is big, because I've got someone who can listen to me, and can support me.

It's all a big part of putting my whole life back together. In my mind, I lost everything, my house, my cars, my money, everything. Mostly, I lost my pride and dignity and those are the hardest things to get back. But when I look back to where I was a year ago stuck in jail and where I am now, I'm starting to get my kids back and I'm getting some of my belongings back, and a lot of things legally have all been in my favor.

That's a blessing, and without God in my life, I don't think all those things would happen. To me, it's been important to get back to my roots, just to see the doors that are opening again. Life is good, and that's the way I have to look at, especially compared to that horrible place I was in my life in jail. Not a day goes by where I don't pray in the evening. Even with all the favorable rulings I'm getting in court – yeah my lawyers have something to do with it – but I think God does, too. The good things that happen, they start there.

34

Chapter

REUNITING AT LONG LAST
WITH MY HOOSIERS

In the summer of 1989, I pulled out of Bloomington to start preparing for my professional career and I never looked back. I had fun playing at Indiana, but when it was time to go, I was ready. I was so glad it was over.

But when I left that summer way back when, I would have never guessed that I would never go back. But that's what happened. I never set foot in Bloomington again until last season, when the current Indiana coach, Tom Crean, opened that door for me. And I'm grateful as hell that he did. It's been so good to be a Hoosier again.

Part of my disconnect, of course, was distance related. During the last ten years of Coach Knight's time at Indiana, I was playing basketball professionally in Europe and then in South America. My seasons ran the same time as Indiana's seasons, so there was no way I could ever be around.

I did come back one time in 1989 to watch the Hoosiers play in Indianapolis at Market Square Arena for the holiday classic. I will never forget it because I was on Christmas break from France and I walked into the locker room before the game and I was dressed from head to toe in leather. I mean, everything. I had a leather jacket and leather pants to match. Coach Knight took one look at me and said "Jadlow, you look like a f------ pimp in a French whore house," Coach brought down the locker room with that statement. I guess he didn't like the leather suit I was wearing. I thought I looked good in it, but Coach thought otherwise.

That was the only time I saw them play, and I never went back to Bloomington. I had so much going on in my life that I didn't even really pay attention to what they were doing. I guess they were really good in 1992 and 1993, but I couldn't tell you one thing about the players on that team.

Even the guys I played with from the fall of 1985 through 1989, I didn't bother keeping in touch with them either. I never talked to Steve Alford or Keith Smart or Dean Garrett. Outside of a few conversations with Mark Robinson, I had absolutely no contact with my former teammates, and I'll be honest, it didn't matter

When Coach Knight was in Kansas City to broadcast a game for ESPN, I caught up with him beforehand. When he said he wasn't going to the 25-year reunion at Indiana, I decided I wasn't going either. I regret that now.

to me one bit.

That, frankly, is a huge regret these days.

When Coach Knight got fired, I didn't talk to him. But I can tell you this. For all my time complaining about how I was treated by Coach Knight, I also took a lot of positives from him that I've used to live my life since then. I am a Coach Knight player, and I don't mind saying that. I am damn proud to be a Coach Knight player.

So when he got fired, I basically cut all ties to Indiana and had nothing to do with them because I was on Coach Knight's side. Mike Davis was the coach for all those years and I never met him nor ever cared about whether they won or lost. It was the same thing when Kelvin Sampson was the coach, and I didn't care when Tom Crean was hired either. I resented Indiana for how they treated Coach Knight, and I had nothing to do with them.

One character flaw I have is that I still have a hard time letting go of stuff. That's one of the things I took from Coach Knight that's not a good thing, and I don't mind admitting that either. I let resentments fuel me. If somebody crosses me once, I just eliminate them, and I got that from Coach, no doubt about it. Being gone for all those years after Coach got fired, that was my resentment to Indiana because of Coach. Coach has a hard time letting things go, too, obviously.

When I was living in Kansas City, I would see Coach Knight every once in a while when he was broadcasting Big 12 games for ESPN. We had a few nice conversations, but nothing deep, and we met for lunch a few times. I saw him a few months before the 25-year reunion for our 1987 national championship team. I asked him if he was going back for it, and he just looked at me and rolled his eyes. So I said, "OK, Coach, if you're not going, then I'm not going either."

235

IN THEIR OWN WORDS

Steve Alford, Indiana (1983-87)

I reached out to Indiana when our 25-yaer anniversary was getting close and I thought it was important to do something special, whether Coach (Knight) was going to be there or not.

I think we all wish Coach would come back, and a lot of players still stand behind him and won't come back. Todd didn't come in 2012 out of loyalty to Coach, and I don't have a problem with guys who decide to do that. I really don't. Everybody handles it differently and I was never in favor of how it went down either. For me, I am an Indiana alum and I'm proud of Indiana University. I've been back a lot, especially when I coached at Iowa, so it's never been a problem for me.

Coach is my mentor, always has been and always will be. He's always had an open door for me throughout my career and I've always appreciated that. I went to IU because of Coach Knight. I went to his camp when I was in the third grade and I went every year. He'll always mean the world to me, just like he does for the rest of the guys. I know how much he means to Todd, too.

I still have endless love for Indiana and I support my school. It's still a score I look for every game.

Steve Alford is currently the head basketball coach at UCLA

I really regret that now because from what I heard, it was a really good night in 2012. I read the articles about it the Blooming-ton newspaper, and I was surprised to see that my name was down on the bottom of a list of players from that team. I was redshirted, but I was still part of that team. They invited me by letter and by e-mail, but I just ignored them all. I probably just threw any letters in the trash.

What did it say about me in the paper? "Whereabouts unknown." I can't fault anyone for that but me, of course, because I probably ignored them. But I was right there in Kansas City in 2012, living the life. The night of the big celebration in Bloom-ington, I was probably drunk or high – or both – surrounded by cocaine and a bunch of women.

A few of my teammates tracked me down after that and wondered why I didn't come. They reminded me that I will always be a part of that team, even though I didn't play that year because I was redshirting. But at that point in my life, I really couldn't care less anyway.

Indiana basketball is truly all about family and about the fans at Indiana University. Too often I think I got caught up in the fact that Coach Knight was the one and only reason why I went to Indiana, and he was the only person there who mattered to me. But when I had all that time to think in jail and when I got out, I started thinking a lot about how much I missed all those guys and needed to reconnect. The more I thought about missing that celebration in 2012, the more I know I can't do that anymore. It said Indiana on my jersey, not Knight.

It's been a long time now since Coach Knight was at Indiana and life goes on. For far too long, I didn't have anything to do with Indiana, but I'm glad that all changed. It all came together after I did a radio interview with Kent Sterling in Indianapolis.

When I made my Senior Night speech in 1989, I would have never guessed it would be 26 years before I would come back to Bloomington.

238

During that interview, he mentioned something about the celebration of the 1976 team that was coming up. I talked to Mark Robinson and he gave me Coach Crean's number and I texted him. It was just a whim, going back to Bloomington. It had been way too long.

Coach Crean called me back right away, and we set up a time for me to come to Bloomington. I went with Rich Castanias to the '76 celebration, and that was something really special. Coach Crean invited me to practice and getting back in the loop was important to me, so that made it a great trip. Scott Dolson, who was a manager back when I played, works in the athletic department and it was great catching up with him, too.

Indiana to me now becomes as important as when I played. There was no reason to be holding any resentments or any grudges any more. I went into Assembly Hall and there was no one around. I knocked on the door and Tim Garl, the trainer who's been around since my days, was there, and he didn't even recognize me at first. I went to practice the next day and Coach had the team come over and introduce them to me. I didn't realize Coach Crean and I were basically the same age and we know a lot of the same people. It was a great first meeting. We didn't really talk about my whole story that first meeting. It wasn't the time.

I did go back to Bloomington after the season and it was great. Coach Crean invited me to talk to his players in April and it was something really special, meeting with all of them in Cook Hall – which is fabulous, by the way – and me telling my whole story to them. I think it really sunk in pretty well. I was also given the chance to speak to several hundred other IU athletes one night at Memorial Hall in the football stadium, and there was a lot of great interaction that night, too. It was good to be back in Bloomington.

What I came to realize after my first few trips back to

239

Bloomington is that Indiana basketball is truly bigger than any one person, any one coach, any one team or any one player. I am truly honored and blessed to have been part of Indiana basketball, the program, its history and to be affiliated with Indiana University. I know there was a time that I wasn't because of everything that had gone on with Coach Knight. There was no way that whole situation was handled right, but what I have come to realize is that holding resentments and grudges doesn't do anybody any good.

Certainly, Coach Knight staying away all these years doesn't do any good for anybody. Certainly not to myself or to anybody I played with. Everyone involved in that mess with Indiana and Coach Knight is long gone now, so why can't we all just move on? Why can't Coach Knight move on? Sometimes I just wish Coach Knight would move on, too. He was a huge part to the success of the Indiana basketball program for well over thirty years. It's my hope that one day he will realize that as great as Indiana basketball is, it's truly about the state and the fans and the people.

Coach Crean and his staff have done a wonderful job of implementing the family back into the program. He told me there is always an open door to come to practices, go to games and come into the locker room anytime. Hats off to him for trying to keep the family together. I was at that 1976 reunion in January of 2016 and it was great. You could see how much the players on that team loved that, and it was a shame that Coach Knight chose not to be a part of it. That's really sad to me.

***   ***   ***

I have started to reconnect with a lot of the former players from my day, too. It's a weird feeling getting back together with those guys because I haven't seen any of them since I left. It's been a complete disconnect. Mark Robinson was the only guy I've kept in touch with.

Playing for Coach was so demanding and so hard, that I kind of liken it to being in the military and then coming back from Iraq or whatever and just feeling the sense of accomplishment about being done. I know in my mind, I was just so glad it was over. Coach always had us keep notebooks during the season, and we would make notes in it every day with things to work on and things to remember. My senior year, we used it to count down the days until it was all over, too.

And when I left, I left. It was so intense, that when I left, I was glad it was done.

We've all gotten together a couple of times this year for various events, and it's been great to be a part of it again. It's nice to reconnect and become friends again. That's been one of the great things about this first year of putting my life back together.

I'm happy to be a Hoosier.

35

Chapter

FIGHTING FOR
MY KIDS GOING FORWARD

My **two oldest daughters** Alexia and Adriana are in their early 20s now and doing well. They've grown into great young adults and I'm very proud of them. My younger two, they live with me a lot of the time now and we have a blast together, even though we have to keep working through an issue or two. This first year out of jail has been a learning experience for all of us, but we're getting there, and I'm excited with what the future brings for all of them. Being a good father to them has always been the one thing that matters the most to me in life.

And then there's my little Camryn, my 5-year-old. I love that little girl to death, and she loves being with me, too. Since I got out of jail, I have basically spent most of that time in court trying to get custody of her again. It's taken a lot of time – and all of my money for lawyers – to have her in my life all the time again. It took me three months of fighting with my ex-wife Nancy just to get her to comply to court orders for me to see Camryn. It's a constant fight, and that's a battle I will never stop fighting with her pain-in-the-butt mother.

She was in the car with me when I was arrested that day, back on December 11, 2013. When they arrested me, my sister

243

came and picked her up and her mother got her a few hours later. From that minute on, my ex-wife Nancy has done everything in her power to keep her away from me. She was the one responsible for that huge media presence at all my court hearings and she's tried to make all of this as public as she can. That first year in jail, I didn't see her at all. The second year, when I was in the therapeutic community, I started the process of getting my child back and getting my custodial rights back. It's been a daily battle.

It started with working through a family services center called TFI and getting monitored visits with her. It took Nancy three months to agree to that, and she even did that reluctantly until she realized finally that there was no way she could keep me away forever. When I first got to see her in March 2015, it didn't go well because she hadn't seen me in 16 months and she was mad

The best thing about getting my life back together is to be around my five wonderful daughters again. This is our family picture from 2016.

at me for leaving her. She only stayed a few seconds and said "No, Daddy. No, Daddy." That just broke my heart. But we kept at it with family services and every visit got a little better.

The visits started taking place more regularly and we'd have an hour and a half together. We'd play with her dolls and do things, and she was starting to get more and more comfortable with each visit. After that I started getting monitored visits with her at my house, and that was great because that's when she really started to get comfortable with me again. We had a great time. We have this incredibly tight bond because we've done everything together since she was born, outside of my time in jail. She was definitely a Daddy's girl. We were together a lot because I wasn't working at the time and I had 50 percent custody before my troubles, so we spent a lot of our days together.

It seemed like every time that we had a court date, where I was trying to get more custodial and parental rights, Nancy would come up with an argument to keep me away. She lied in court so many times. It's all about money to her. She thinks that she'll get more money if she has her more, but that's not going to happen. I've always been a great dad, even though I know I messed up and went through that hard battle.

My kids have always come first. Going through all of this in the past year has been incredibly expensive. All told, it's probably getting close to $100,000 in expenses just to get through this legal process. Every time there was a court date for something to get settled, it would get pushed back for one reason or another that she would come up with. First in was March, then May and then October. It just goes on and on. I have done everything that has been asked of me, from counseling to parenting classes. I keep getting more and more time, even though it's still not nearly enough. When they first increased my parenting time, I would get her on

Fridays at 6 p.m. and I would have her till Sunday at 6 p.m. Even then, someone from the program stops into my house a couple of times on the weekend to check on us. Camryn is always fine. She loves it with me and she just adores being around all her big sisters. They love her, too.

Going through a child custody battle is horrible, as anyone who's been through it knows. I created this situation and this mess and there are two things I can do: I can either walk away from it and wash my hands of it all, which I see happen often because it is extremely emotional and extremely tough financially for a lot of people. It's just never-ending so I can certainly understand why parents – or one of the parents – say "I can't do this anymore" and just have to walk away. It's also so expensive. I've basically used every penny that I've had in my life savings to try to correct the wrong that I did.

The thing I choose to do is to never quit fighting for my children. Going through this is horrible, and I wouldn't wish it on my worst enemy. But I will never quit fighting.

I would never forgive myself if I did not try to correct this. I will get my daughter back. The final decision will come from the judge, but I'm ready for it to happen. I'm confident in a good result because I have done everything right since I got out of jail to make sure it does. I am a good father and I love my kids, all five of them.

I cherish every single minute I get with them, no matter what it is we are doing. It means even more to me now, after all of this. Every day is great.

So will all the tomorrows.

36

Chapter

FIGHTING FOR MY FUTURE BY
DOING THE RIGHT THINGS EVERY DAY

I have a lot of challenges staring me in the face now as I move forward, but the biggest challenge for me here at the end of 2016 is getting some stability in my life. Playing for Coach Knight at Indiana was like being in the military. Everything was structured, A to B to C. I have always lived my life like that, with the exception of the last five years. That's just me, and I like living that way with structure and organization in my life. I have to live by a routine, and be in a happy place. It's a must. So I'm asking myself all the time, how do I improve? What do I need to do to get better?.

Right now, I'll be honest, I'm in limbo. At some point, I'm hoping my Foundation becomes my routine. Five years from now, I hope I have something steady that I enjoy doing every day. My goal is to get it to a point where we have outside people doing all the little things, and all I do is focus on talking to people, and helping as many people as I can.

I'm looking forward to getting it growing quickly, so we can help people in a lot of places. We have a saying in basketball that you're only as good as the last game you played. So it's true for me now, too. Every speech I give, it has to be good, because it can lead to the next one and the one after that. I need to stay out there and keep telling my story.

Right now, I'm still just in survival mode. That's where I am. It's hard, but it takes me back to what it was like being an Indiana basketball player. I thrive on structure, and I always have and that takes me all the way back to Coach Knight and my time in Bloomington. Right now, sometimes I feel like I'm a rogue soldier, starting this from scratch. At IU, everything was regimented right down to the last second, and I want to get back to being in that kind of structure. I have always lived my life that way. If I had to be somewhere at 1 o'clock, I wasn't getting there at 1, I was getting there at 12:50.

That all changed after the car wreck, when my head got wobbly and I started making bad decisions. I've been wandering

There's no way I could have made it without Jamie. She's been my rock.

ever since. Several times I would drink so much and take all those pills and really hope that I wouldn't wake up the next day. It was that bad. I was ready to die. I completely closed people out and quit socializing and isolated myself. I would hide and drink myself silly. I would just stay at home and drink, or go to other people's house and drink.

I definitely don't want to ever live that way again. I want to build something, live my life, take care of my kids, love again – this time the right way – and keep moving forward.

I'm grateful to have a few people around – the right kind of people this time – to help give me structure, but it's still a learning process to sort of start my life all over again. My beautiful girlfriend Jamie, has been a huge, huge help in my progress. My kids, too. Having people helping me with my Foundation is great, too. It's a good mix of people, and they all bring something to the table for me, to help me. They all give me a lot of strength, and it's great to have this structure back in my life.

My goal is to help people who are in need of treatment but can't afford it. We can help people if they need a place to live, or go somewhere like Oxford House or Welcome House, where they can go stay for a while.

We want to help with First Call, and they will help give scholarships to people to help pay for treatment or rehab. And the more we grow, the more people we can help. It's all a learning process. We're new at this, but I want it that way. We worked hard on a mission statement, but we keep it short and sweet. To reach one child, one person or one family, and make a difference in their lives. We want to keep it simple and keep our administrative costs down so we can help more people.

Starting from scratch, it's exciting. Thank God, people are helping me keep it simple. That's the best way for me to live

IN THEIR OWN WORDS

Mike Tompkins, Recovery Director
& Co-Owner of Tompkins Industries

It didn't take long for Todd and I to become fast friends after we started spending some time together. My first encounter with him, when I got in his face, I didn't think he cared much about getting better.

Now I can say unequivocally that he's all about recovery and making a difference in his life.

A lot of our conversations about recovery have had some overtures to his basketball days. You just can't get better without preparation and without working hard at it. Todd knows that now, and he sees it, not only in himself but in others as well.

I've been able to go with Todd to several of his speaking engagements and it's amazing how well he connects with kids when he's talking to them. He reaches them by telling them that he really does hope and pray they don't follow his path of destruction.

For Todd, reaching out to others is also going to be a big part of his own recovery. He talks about it often, and I see it in him as well. I think the more he tells his story, the more he knows he has to do everything the right way now going forward too, or his talks about his experiences don't mean anything to anybody.

People like Todd who have had a lot of success in life often don't know how to deal with adversity when it hits them. He's handling it great, moving forward.

Todd isn't going to let his problems define him. He's made mistakes, and he knows it, but he also knows there's a lot of life still ahead of him. There's plenty more that will still define Todd.

my life. I'm still making the transition. But what's nice is feeling confident about what's coming down the road. When you have an addictive personality, you kind of want everything now, but it's all about learning about getting it back little by little. You need patience, but that's not a virtue I have.

I'm of that nature of wanting to fix a problem, and fix it now, right now. That's not always possible. I leave a lot on the table every day, days that are mental struggles because I'm still dealing with aspects of depression. Some days are still hard to deal with. But at least now I have the ability not to react on those things, to keep going. I don't need to get all drunk or wasted anymore to deal with my depression. Now I know how to do things right.

I've learned a lot, but I have so much more to learn. I've got a lot of flaws, and I'm working on fixing them, little by little.

*** *** ***

It's one thing to fix your issues with drugs and alcohol. That I can do, and I feel good about it. But that hasn't been my only flaw through the years. Ever since I can remember, I've always treated the women in my life terribly. I can honest tell you that I have never been faithful to a single woman in my life. I was married for 15 years, and when I was playing in Argentina, I had a girlfriend there for two years. She lived with me, and when my wife would come over, she would move out. And when my wife would leave, she would move right back in the next day. Sometimes, the same day.

My first wife, she never even liked living with me when I was playing because she hated being by herself when I was on the road. That went on for seven, eight years where we wouldn't even

IN THEIR OWN WORDS

Jamie Carpenter, Todd's NEW FIANCEE

In the last year since Todd has come home, seeing him change his life has been exciting for me. I knew he was capable of change, but I also knew it wasn't going to be easy.

We both have parallel situations because I was coming out of a difficult abusive relationship myself. Todd had jail, but the abuse I went through was my prison too. So when he came home, it certainly wasn't easy because we were both going through a lot of adjustments.

What was so obvious to me was that Todd was sincere about wanting to make a change in his life and fix the things he had messed up for years. He's really trying to make a relationship work now, and that's not something that's always been a priority for him. Now he's putting into action a lot of the things he's talked about changing.

We are truly best friends right now. I know I can confide anything in him and he does the same for me now. That's a big step for both of us, but it works because we have this true, unconditional love for each other.

He asked me to marry him on my birthday and I gladly said yes. We both hold each other accountable every day, and there's just no words to express how emotional this all is, seeing him grow every day. I am very proud of him and all that he's doing right now. I'm glad to be at his side.

Jamie Carpenter and Todd Jadlow became engaged on Oct. 3, 2016 live together. She spent more time with her family in Europe than she did with me. I figured I had the best of both worlds back then. When I played, every city I went to, there would be women they would send up to my room. You would forget about the aspect that you were married. It never bothered me even once. It was always about me.

I've always told people I don't know how people can be with the same person all the time. I say that because I've never really known that feeling in my own life. I can honestly say – not proudly, mind you – that in all the years I was married, I was unfaithful every single year. And after I got divorced, I went from one woman to the next all the time, and they always overlapped. I didn't care. It was all about just having fun.

But now I'm finally realizing the value of a meaningful relationship now that I'm with Jamie and I'm working so hard at it. It sure wasn't my mind-set for years and years. That's not normal either, and I understand that. There's nothing I can really pin that on, nothing growing up that made me have a lack of respect for women. I always had to have women around, and I've had hundreds of girlfriends. It was never necessarily about the sex aspect of it, it was just the company and having people around and the excitement of it all. I can't stand being bored.

Jamie has seen the worst in me and has always been there by my side even when I've been horrible to her and hurt her badly. To this day it still tears me up inside to know how much I have hurt her through the years because of the deep love and appreciation I have for her.

I truly believe that everyone finds that special person in their life at some point, and God has sent Jamie as that person for me. I am grateful that even through all the hell I have put her through, she is still there for me. She has taught me something that

I truly did not believe existed and that is total unconditional love. Without her in my life I can honestly say I don't know where I would be. I am constantly trying to prove to her every day that I am the man that is worthy of her love, and can be honest, devoted and faithful. I can't imagine life without her and don't ever plan on having a life without her.

To have a life with Jamie, I had to completely change several aspects of my life, not only in actions but in thoughts and words as well.

I really don't know about all the long-term effects of all that cocaine on my head. All that, and the alcohol. Jamie tells me stories about things that I did and I don't even remember them. I'll tell her, "You're making that up," and she would just shake her head. She knew it happened, but I didn't remember a bit of it. I worry about the effect it will have on my long-term memory as well. That, and the concussions.

I think in my mind it's easier to change my aspect of thinking on drugs and alcohol than it does changing how I go about treating women. If I got in a fight with a girl before, I'd just say screw it and go on to the next one. That's something I can't do anymore, and I'm still trying to figure that out in my head, too.

The hardest thing for Jamie to understand in the four-plus years we've been together is that through most of it, it's just been Todd being Todd. Those first few years, every time we'd get into arguments, I'd be calling other people, and I can see now how that can be hurtful. But I care so much for her now, because she stood by me through all of this and that really means a lot to me. I can honestly say that I am in love for the first time in my life.

And it feels great.

I'm surrounded by better people now. I can count the number of people I hang around with on one hand. I don't go out. I spend all my time with Jamie or my kids, and that's it. Every friend that I associated with before, they're all out of my life now. All my friends were all about that life, eating and drinking and playing cards, or going on a trip, so I had to eliminate everybody. Everybody was part of that life, the alcohol and drugs.

Jamie is good for me because she has a really strong character and she doesn't play. I can't go back there, because I know the way that story ends. My life isn't full of exciting nights now, but that's a good thing for me. I have a nice balance in my life now and lots of positive things are happening. That's a really good thing for me. I can honestly say I am in love with Jamie, and it's really the first time I have been in love. I never want to lose that. She completes me and she is my person.

***　　***　　***

It's extremely hard for me to go out and tell my story, but at the same time it is very liberating and very freeing for me. I get more good out of me talking than some of the people listening because it keeps me on the right path. It takes a lot of strength to share your weaknesses and wrongdoings in life with people when I've always been extremely quiet through the years. I hate it when my ex-wives will argue in court that I only talk to people because it's all about my ego. It's just not like that at all. I don't go do talks and talk about how great I am. I'm telling the worst, darkest secrets of my life and that's not easy.

I have always struggled with self-esteem issues. Not caring enough about myself had a lot to do with why I put all those drugs and all that alcohol in my body. It's a little different now, because I put myself out there now and show my weaknesses. As an athlete you were always taught to hide all your weaknesses. Self-esteem

255

is a huge issue for me, and it explains a lot about how my behavior has been. It's still not what it should be.

I'm much more open now about the stuff that's brought me down, but it's still a tough pill to swallow to look back at what I've done. And why? That's always a hard question for me to answer. I'm still at the bottom with self-esteem and self-worth, and I think about that on a daily basis. Why do I think different? Why do I act different? And I see that in the kids I talk to. If I can help them feel stronger, that's the most validating part of everything I do right now. Kent Sterling's mom sent me a note after I was on Kent's radio show in Indianapolis, and it brought me to tears. She touched my heart like I had never experienced before. She was telling me she was thinking about me, and what I've been through. We've had a chance to talk on the phone a few times since then and that's been incredible as well. She has a warm heart full of empathy and support, and that means a lot to me.

I get a letter or two after every time I talk. From some schools, I get six or seven or more. When I spoke at Sacred Heart in Salina where I went to high school, one of the girls sent me a letter saying how much my talk meant to her. That was so nice.

And you know what was so ironic? She was the daughter of one of the guys who tortured me about my tics when I was a kid. It took me back full circle. I talked to her a couple of times, and I've talked with people through Facebook or by e-mail after my talks. It's the people who are struggling or need help who reach out, and that's great. I try to get them help. That's what I really want to do going forward. It's my passion now, because I don't ever want anyone to have to go through what I went through. Kids finding an outlet to speak about what's going on, that's what really matters because it opens the door for conversation for a lot of these kids.

The whole key to sharing my story is to try to help prevent someone else from going down the path you went down. It doesn't matter if you are black or white or Hispanic, or if you have money or not, it's about being true to yourself and helping someone not go through what I went through, to lose everything and to be humiliated.

I don't like to talk about how great I'm doing. I want to talk more about how I've changed as a person and how I got there. Everything that I thought was important to me has been stripped away from me, and in essence I'm starting all over, but there's nothing boastful about that.

I'm just trying to help somebody else now, and if I do that, then it's all worth it. If I'm going to talk that talk, then I'm walking that walk. And that's good for me, too.

Talk the talk, and walk the walk.

I'm good with that.

***   ***   ***

Part of doing the right things and getting better is being able to enjoy all the good things that start coming back into your life. I've talked a lot about how much my girlfriend Jamie has helped me on this long journey through the good and the bad.

For more than four years, we've had a lot of ups and downs. Our love has really grown strong these past few years, and I could never be where I am today without her.

When the subject of marriage has come up, one thing that Jamie always said was that I would never be able to surprise her. But as the clock struck midnight on Oct. 3, I went into her house in Overland Park on a mission. She was sleeping, and I startled her when I came in. She asked me what I was doing coming over at midnight, and I told her I needed to talk to her. We had been bickering a lot of the day – something I instigated, by design – and I'm sure she felt I wanted to talk about that.

I sat down on the bed and gave her a birthday card, since she had just turned 40 at midnight. While she was reading the card, I opened a box and there it was, a beautiful diamond ring that I had spent months designing and making perfect. I asked her to marry me. Her hands were literally shaking uncontrollably when she saw the ring.

I had done it. I had surprised her and caught her completely off guard. I'm not the most romantic guy on the planet, and I often search for the right words to say at the right time. But this moment? I was speechless, and so was she. Then she said yes, of course, and we both sat there literally in shock. Our fate was sealed.

I truly consider myself the luckiest man on earth because I have found my true soul mate, the woman I was meant to spend the rest of my life with, a woman that I was meant to care for and love the rest of my life.

It's been four-and-a-half years since Jamie and I first met and I can honestly say I have put her through hell with everything I have done in my life, but she's been there through thick and thin.

I can't imagine my life with Jamie and now I won't ever have to worry about that. I love her today and tomorrow, always and forever.

About the Todd Jadlow Give It Back Foundation

If you would like Todd Jadlow to speak at your next event or are interested in making a foundation donation, please contact the foundation at: **giveitbackfoundation@gmail.com**

**Follow all foundation
activities on Facebook.**

**A portion of the proceeds from the
sale of this book benefits the
Todd Jadlow Give It Back Foundation**

Author's Note

For more than 40 years, I've had the pleasure of writing about college basketball in and around Indiana, but in the past 22 years I've also enjoyed tackling the issues of addiction and recovery in my writing and speaking.

In the past two years, I have written two books, one a novel called "The Ties That Bind" that deals with gambling addiction in college athletes and another called "Missing Banners" that deals with some lost seasons of Indiana University basketball.

And then along comes Todd Jadlow. Todd and I first touched base early in 2016 when I was touring with the release of "Missing Banners" and he was getting reacquainted with Indiana University after a 26-year hiatus away from Bloomington.

Todd told me he had a great story to tell himself and we started discussing it. What Todd didn't know at the time was that I had my own history of ruining lives and then finding recovery. I've spent 22 years recovering from a gambling addiction and I've worked with hundreds of addicts since then.

With Todd, our hundreds of hours of interviews and conversations over the past six months have been more than writer and source. It's also been a lot of tear-soaked conversations for both us, about what we've lost, what we've endured and what we wish for the future.

It's been really good for both of us.

What I love about this book is that Todd has been brutally honest throughout. Part of that, he's admitted in interviews with others, is that he knew he couldn't spin things the wrong way with me, because I've heard all the stories from people in recovery before. I know the lies, the deceit, the fakery. We didn't have any of that. Todd knows he can't toss bull crap at me, because I have heard it all before. I hold him to a high standard, too.

So what's left is a heartwrenching story of a life lived on the edge, and the hard work that's involved in turning his life around. I have an enormous amount of respect for the work Todd has done on his recovery, and how he's worked very hard to getting back to being a great father to his five daughters, whom I've had the pleasure to spend some time with as well.

This project has been a great experience for me and I hope you like it. I also hope you share Todd's story with anyone you know who is battling -- or has battled -- issues with drugs or alcohol or gambling addictions.

What you've learned -- we both hope -- from Todd's story is that it's more about fixing the person inside than it is the chemicals or the actions that medicate and destroy it. We sure hope this story finds its way to the right people. We both hope you help us spread the word.

Thanks for reading.

Tom Brew

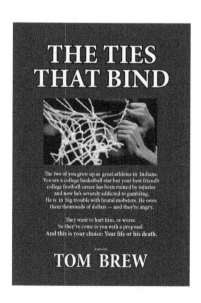 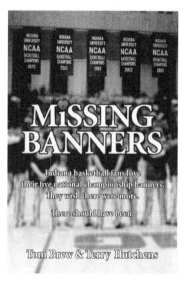

To order copies of this book or any others from Tom Brew, email him at tombrew@hilltop30.com

*Hilltop30 Publishers, LLC *** Schererville, Indiana*

Made in the USA
Coppell, TX
25 May 2020

26398614R10148